THE CHRYSOSTOM BIBLE
A Commentary Series for Preaching and Teaching
Genesis: A Commentary

THE CHRYSOSTOM BIBLE

A Commentary Series for Preaching and Teaching

Genesis: A Commentary

Paul Nadim Tarazi

OCABS PRESS
ST PAUL, MINNESOTA 55112
2009

THE CHRYSOSTOM BIBLE
GENESIS: A COMMENTARY

ISBN 1-60191-008-8

PRINTED IN THE UNITED STATES OF AMERICA

For Archbishop Philip Saliba
another bishop of the church
from Antioch

Other Books by the Author

I Thessalonians: A Commentary

Galatians: A Commentary

The Old Testament: An Introduction

Volume 1: Historical Traditions, revised edition

Volume 2: Prophetic Traditions

Volume 3: Psalms and Wisdom

The New Testament: An Introduction

Volume 1: Paul and Mark

Volume 2: Luke and Acts

Volume 3: Johannine Writings

Volume 4: Matthew and the Canon

The Chrysostom Bible
Genesis: A Commentary

ISBN 1-60191-008-8

Published by OCABS Press, St. Paul, Minnesota.
Printed in the United States of America.

Books are available through OCABS Press at special discounts
for bulk purchases in the United States by academic institutions,
churches, and other organizations. For more information please
email OCABS Press at press@ocabs.org.

Abbreviations

Books by the Author

1 Thess   *I Thessalonians: A Commentary,* Crestwood, NY: St. Vladimir's Seminary
Press, 1982

Gal   *Galatians: A Commentary,* Crestwood, NY: St. Vladimir's Seminary Press,
1994

OTI_1 *The Old Testament: An Introduction, Volume 1: Historical Traditions,*
revised edition, Crestwood, NY: St. Vladimir's Seminary Press, 2003

OTI_2 *The Old Testament: An Introduction, Volume 2: Prophetic Traditions,*
Crestwood, NY: St. Vladimir's Seminary Press, 1994

OTI_3 *The Old Testament: An Introduction, Volume 3: Psalms and Wisdom,*
Crestwood, NY: St. Vladimir's Seminary Press, 1996

NTI_1 *The New Testament: An Introduction, Volume 1: Paul and Mark,*
Crestwood, NY: St. Vladimir's Seminary Press, 1999

NTI_2 *The New Testament: An Introduction, Volume 2: Luke and Acts,* Crestwood,
NY: St. Vladimir's Seminary Press, 2001

NTI_3 *The New Testament: An Introduction, Volume 3: Johannine Writings,*
Crestwood, NY: St. Vladimir's Seminary Press, 2004

NTI_4 *The New Testament: An Introduction, Volume 4: Matthew and the Canon,*
St. Paul, MN: OCABS Press, 2009

Abbreviations

*Books of the Old Testament**

Gen	Genesis	Job	Job	Hab	Habakkuk	
Ex	Exodus	Ps	Psalms	Zeph	Zephaniah	
Lev	Leviticus	Prov	Proverbs	Hag	Haggai	
Num	Numbers	Eccl	Ecclesiastes	Zech	Zechariah	
Deut	Deuteronomy	Song	Song of Solomon	Mal	Malachi	
Josh	Joshua	Is	Isaiah	Tob	Tobit	
Judg	Judges	Jer	Jeremiah	Jdt	Judith	
Ruth	Ruth	Lam	Lamentations	Wis	Wisdom	
1 Sam	1 Samuel	Ezek	Ezekiel	Sir	Sirach (Ecclesiasticus)	
2 Sam	2 Samuel	Dan	Daniel	Bar	Baruch	
1 Kg	1 Kings	Hos	Hosea	1 Esd	1 Esdras	
2 Kg	2 Kings	Joel	Joel	2 Esd	2 Esdras	
1 Chr	1 Chronicles	Am	Amos	1 Macc	1 Maccabees	
2 Chr	2 Chronicles	Ob	Obadiah	2 Macc	2 Maccabees	
Ezra	Ezra	Jon	Jonah	3 Macc	3 Maccabees	
Neh	Nehemiah	Mic	Micah	4 Macc	4 Maccabees	
Esth	Esther	Nah	Nahum			

Books of the New Testament

Mt	Matthew	Eph	Ephesians	Heb	Hebrews
Mk	Mark	Phil	Philippians	Jas	James
Lk	Luke	Col	Colossians	1 Pet	1 Peter
Jn	John	1 Thess	1 Thessalonians	2 Pet	2 Peter
Acts	Acts	2 Thess	2 Thessalonians	1 Jn	1 John
Rom	Romans	1 Tim	1 Timothy	2 Jn	2 John
1 Cor	1 Corinthians	2 Tim	2 Timothy	3 Jn	3 John
2 Cor	2 Corinthians	Titus	Titus	Jude	Jude
Gal	Galatians	Philem	Philemon	Rev	Revelation

Following the larger canon known as the Septuagint.

Contents

Preface

The present Bible Commentary Series is not so much in honor of John Chrysostom as it is to continue and promote his legacy as an interpreter of the biblical texts for preaching and teaching God's congregation, in order to prod its members to proceed on the way they started when they accepted God's calling. Chrysostom's virtual uniqueness is that he did not subscribe to any hermeneutic or methodology, since this would amount to introducing an extra-textual authority over the biblical texts. For him, scripture is its own interpreter. Listening to the texts time and again allowed him to realize that "call" and "read (aloud)" are not interconnected realities; rather, they are one reality since they both are renditions of the same Hebrew verb *qara'*. Given that words read aloud are words of instruction for one "to do them," the only valid reaction would be to hear, listen, obey, and abide by these words. All these connotations are subsumed in the same Hebrew verb *šama'*. On the other hand, these scriptural "words of life" are presented as readily understandable utterances of a father to his children (Isaiah 1:2-3). The recipients are never asked to engage in an intellectual debate with their divine instructor, or even among themselves, to fathom what he is saying. The Apostle to the Gentiles followed in the footsteps of the Prophets to Israel by handing down to them the Gospel, that is, the Law of God's Spirit through his Christ (Romans 8:2; Galatians 6:2) as fatherly instruction (1 Corinthians 4:15). He in turn wrote readily understandable letters to be read aloud. It is in these same footsteps that Chrysostom followed, having learned from both the Prophets and Paul that the same "words of life" carry also the sentence of death at the hand of the scriptural God, Judge of all

(Deuteronomy 28; Joshua 8:32-35; Psalm 82; Matthew 3:4-12; Romans 2:12-16; 1 Corinthians 10:1-11; Revelation 20:11-15).

While theological debates and hermeneutical theories come and go after having fed their proponents and their fans with passing human glory, the Golden Mouth's expository homilies, through the centuries, fed and still feed myriads of believers in so many traditions and countries. Virtually banned from dogmatic treatises, he survives in the hearts of "those who have ears to hear." His success is due to his commitment to exegesis rather than to futile hermeneutics. The latter behaves as someone who dictates on a living organism what it is supposed to be, whereas exegesis submits to that organism and endeavors to decipher it through trial and error. There is as much a far cry between the text and the theories about it as there is between a living organism and the theories about it. The biblical texts are the reality of God imparted through their being read aloud in the midst of the congregation, disregarding the value of the sermon that follows. The sermon, much less a theological treatise, is at best an invitation to hear and obey the text. Assessing the shape of an invitation card has no value whatsoever when it comes to the dinner itself; the guests are fed by the dinner, not by the invitation or its phrasing (Luke 14:16-24; Matthew 22:1-14).

This commentary series does not intend to promote Chrysostom's ideas as a public relation manager would do, but rather to follow in the footsteps of his approach as true children and heirs are expected to do. He used all the contemporary tools at his disposal to communicate God's written instruction to his hearers, as a doctor would with his patients, without spending unnecessary energy on peripheral debates requiring the use of professional jargon incomprehensible to the commoner. The writers of this series will try to do the same: muster to the best of their ability all necessary contemporary knowledge to communicate to the general readers the biblical message without burdening them with data unnecessary for that purpose. Whenever it will be deemed necessary or even helpful to do so, and in order to curtail burdensome and lengthy technical asides within the commentaries, specialized monographs related either to specific topics or to the scriptural background—literary, sociopolitical, or archeological—will be issued as companions to the series.

Paul Nadim Tarazi
Editor

Introduction

Traditionally, the Old Testament consists of three parts: the Law (Torah), the Prophets, and the (other) Writings. The Torah is actually the basis on which the life of the Israelites in Canaan, dealt with in the Prophets, is judged. Although the first part of scripture is referred to as the Law, the actual legal texts are found in the last four books (Exodus, Leviticus, Numbers, and Deuteronomy). The first book, Genesis, deals with what may be considered as the human story that leads to the necessity for and the rise of the law issued by God through Moses. Already St. John Chrysostom, to whom this commentary series is dedicated, captured the reality of this matter:

> It were indeed meet for us not at all to require the aid of the written Word, but to exhibit a life so pure, that the grace of the Spirit should be instead of books to our souls, and that as these are inscribed with ink, even so should our hearts be with the Spirit. But, since we have utterly put away from us this grace, come, let us at any rate embrace the second best course. For that the former was better, God hath made manifest, both by His words, and by His doings, since unto Noah, and unto Abraham, and unto his offspring, and unto Job, and unto Moses too, He discoursed not by writings, but Himself by Himself, finding their mind pure. But after the whole people of the Hebrews had fallen into the very pit of wickedness, then and thereafter was a written word, and tables, and the admonition which is given by these.[1]

Consequently, the Book of Genesis sets the tone for the entire scripture. It defines the biblical vocabulary as well as introduces the plot of the biblical story. In a sense, it can be considered as

---

[1] Homily I on the Gospel of St. Matthew in P. Schaff, ed., *The Nicene and Post-Nicene Fathers* (Grand Rapids, 1st Series, x 1978).

the institutional or constitutional scriptural book. Both its titles
"In the beginning" (Hebrew) and "Genesis" (Greek) are actually
more than apt if one takes them in the sense that the book opens
up as well as opens to the hearers the scripture as literature. We
have to recapture that original function of the Bible. It is first
and foremost a literary story that has a beginning and an end
beyond which one may not venture backward nor creatively
push forward. Any such endeavor is adding to the scroll that
"had writing on the front and on the back" and which was
spread out to the divine prophets by God's own hand (Ezek 2:8-
10) to the extent that those prophets uttered the words that God
himself put in their mouths (Jer 1:9). Indeed, God may have
done or said other things to which, we were told, we shall never
be privy, the reason being that such additions would be
unnecessary and thus potentially detrimental for God's plan of
inviting us into his kingdom: "Now Jesus did many other signs
in the presence of the disciples, which are not written in this
book; but these are written that you may believe that Jesus is the
Christ, the Son of God, and that believing you may have life in
his name." (Jn 20:30-31)[2] The reason behind the express
prohibition to subtract from or add to the scriptural text is that
the realities referred to in it are intra-textual and not extra-
textual: "I solemnly testify to (and thus against) everyone who
hears the words of the prophecy of this book: if any one adds to
them, God will add to him the plagues *which are written in this
book*, and if any one takes away from the words of the book of
this prophecy, God will take away his share in the tree of life and
in the holy city, *which are written in this book*." (Rev 22:18-19)

---

[2] Actually, adding to scripture would prove an impossible task: "But there are also
many other things which Jesus did; were every one of them to be written, I suppose
that the world itself could not contain the books that would be written." (Jn 21:25)

That is why, in our tradition, the central services of baptism (and the great blessing of the waters as well) and eucharist revolve around a lengthy and detailed commemoration of the biblical story. Unless the recollection of God is done in this manner, the attendees may risk ending up in the presence of an idol and not the living God. In other words, God becomes alive in our midst when we are pulled *into* the biblical story and not when we venture to extract him *out of* it. May the readers of the present volume find it helpful in having introduced them *into* the "beginnings" of that saving odyssey!

Part I

The Creation Narratives

1

Toledot

The biblical story spanning Genesis 1-11 is divided into substories entitled *toledot* (Gen 2:4; 5:1; 6:9; 10:1, 32; 11:10, 27).[1] This term is from the root *yalad* (to give birth, to engender, as mammals do), and thus refers to the progeny of the person whose *toledot* the text is dealing with. However, the term has definitely a technical ring to it since it is used in conjunction with "the heavens and the earth" in 2:4. Thus, it is imperative to clear the matter before engaging into the actual story. Actually, the correct understanding of the biblical story hinges on a precise understanding of what *toledot* means.

A close look at the stories will readily show that a person's first mention occurs in the *toledot* of his progenitor, meaning that his individual being is part and parcel of the progenitor's *toledot*, whereas that person's own *toledot* looks ahead, as it were. In this regard, my readers' attention is drawn to the fact that Abraham's biblical story evolves within and under the umbrella of his father Terah's *toledot* (Gen 11:27). The story of Noah's sons is under the heading of Noah's *toledot* (Gen 6:9-9:29), while the *toledot* of each son is the umbrella title for the children of each (Gen 10:1, 2, 7, 20, 21-22, 31; 11:10). This aspect, in and of itself, raises a red flag of caveat against the use of the classical philosophical and theological anthropology that looks at the individual as

---

[1] I am using the Hebrew term on purpose because the translations usually blur the original.

sandwiched between birth and death, having a value in and of himself without reference to the larger social setting: family, clan, tribe. This philosophic-anthropological stand, in turn, coupled with our ego, became the basis of positing a soul that is self-standing and thus extendable into a life beyond death. Such is not the biblical way. The individual is rather subsumed in the seed (Hebrew *zera'*, Greek *sperma*), and thus *toledot* of the forebear. Put otherwise, the individual is an expression of the progenitor's seed. If so, then one's own personal story and thus value lies in whether one's seed is fruitful or not.[2] That is why the biblical *toledot* of an individual opens up a new chapter, the story of that individual's progeny, his own "after-story," as it were.[3] The corollary is that the potentiality itself of someone having a *toledot* is rooted in that person's having been part of someone else's *toledot*. In other words, one is essentially as well as primarily the product of a "seed," one is already posited as a premise. This rule applies in the Bible even to the so-called "first human being": Adam's *toledot* is relegated to Genesis 5:1! Genesis 1-4 is not the story of Adam (and Eve), let alone of Cain and Abel; it is rather the *toledot* of the heavens and the earth, Adam being merely the product, the fruit, of the latter: "then the Lord God formed the man (human being)[4] of dust from the ground (*'adamah*), and breathed into his nostrils the breath of life; and man became a living being." (Gen 2:7) One notices that the ground (of the earth [*'ereṣ*]) is the grammatical feminine

---

[2] One is reminded of the Lord's statement in Mt 7:17-20 (So, every sound tree bears good fruit, but the bad tree bears evil fruit. A sound tree cannot bear evil fruit, nor can a bad tree bear good fruit. Every tree that does not bear good fruit is cut down and thrown into the fire. Thus you will know them by their fruits) as well as of the Baptist's threat in Mt 3:10 (Even now the axe is laid to the root of the trees; every tree therefore that does not bear good fruit is cut down and thrown into the fire).

[3] The Arabic adage is telling: "Whoever begets is not dead."

[4] The original Hebrew reads *ha'adam* (the man), with the definite article.

'adamah of the Hebrew masculine *'adam*,[5] thus functioning as the latter's progenitor "mother." The conclusion imposes itself: Genesis 1-4 is the "story" (*toledot*) of the heavens and the earth (Gen 2:4) and not that of Adam. Hence, the classical "anthropological" reading of those chapters is to be discarded as not being an exegesis, but rather an *eisegesis* (reading unwarranted meaning into) which is the product of our egotistic anthropocentrism whose most powerful expression is the Platonic premise of the self-standing (eternal) soul.

The toledot *of the Heavens and the Earth*

How should one understand the apparently oxymoronic statement "the *toledot* of the heavens and the earth" (Gen 2:4)? How could one speak of the "generation" (as in procreation) of something inanimate? The only plausible solution is to conclude, as I mentioned earlier, that the term *toledot* is used functionally as meaning "the coming about of something." However, the answer cannot be so simplistic since the text itself mentions in that same verse the verb "create" (*bara*) that was used in Genesis 1:1:

> In the beginning God *created* (*bara*) the heavens and the earth. (Gen 1:1)

> These are the generations (*toledot*) of the heavens and the earth *when they were created* (*behibbare'am*). (Gen 2:4a)

So the question remains, "Why would the author have wanted to use also the term *toledot* and, more specifically, as the subject of the sentence, relegating the verb *bara'* to a subordinate clause?" Put otherwise, why would he give in 2:4 the ascendancy to the idea of begetting over that of creating, which refers to the main

---

[5] Hebrew has only two grammatical genders, the masculine and the feminine.

action in 1:1? Or even, why did he not simply start his story in
1:1 with the words: "These are the generations of the heavens
and the earth when God created them"?

The solution lies in the meaning and function of *toledot*. To
speak of the *toledot* (literally "birth") of heavens and earth, the
cycle will have continued ad infinitum. In order to avoid this
dilemma, the author links heavens and earth to their producer,
God, through a different verb than *yalad* (give birth). The verb
he uses, *bara'*, is one whose subject is always God in scripture,
making of it a specifically divine action. This specificity is at its
clearest in a later text, where though the result of the action is
the same, yet the action itself is expressed through two different
verbs: "This is the book of the *toledot* of Adam. When God
created (from the root *bara'*) Adam, he made him in the likeness
of God… When Adam had lived a hundred and thirty years, he
gave birth to (from the root *yalad*) a son in his own likeness, after
his image, and named him Seth." (Gen 5:1, 3) Furthermore, the
author put a literary chasm between God's action (Gen 1:1) and
the *toledot* of heavens and earth by relegating the latter to
Genesis 2:4a at the juncture of the two creation narratives (Gen
1:1-2:3 and 2:4b-3:24). Finally, through the addition of the
subordinate clause "when they (the heavens and the earth) were
created" to the classic title "These are the *toledot* of the heavens
and the earth," he actually fully subordinated these *toledot* to
God's action just as he will later subordinate the *toledot* of Adam
to that same action (Gen 5:1-3).

The Meaning of the Hebrew bara'

What is the meaning of *bara'*? This Semitic root has the
connotation of healing, mending, bringing (back) someone or
something to a healthy, sane, viable state. In other words, *bara'*

means (re)habilitate, make functional someone or something that is or has been brought into a status of mere appearance, but without functional being. The opposite of such a state is desolation or rubble, the Hebrew *tohu wabohu* (Gen 1:2), as is clear from the prophetic texts where either *tohu* or *bohu* occurs.[6] That *tohu*[7] is the status of the earth requiring the divine action reflected in *bara'* is at its clearest in Second Isaiah (Is 40-55), the prophet of the restoration pursuant to desolation, where we encounter the highest incidence of both *tohu* and *bara'*.[8] This, in turn, explains why Genesis 1:2 is a nominal sentence describing the status of the earth *before* God intervened in v.3 and not a sentence initiated by a *waw consecutive*, which would have indicated that v.2 was the result of the divine *bara'* of v.1. The latter stance, scripturally speaking, would be oxymoronic: desolation is divine punishment of something that used to be functional, whereas *bara'* connotes a divine restorative action. Consequently, God could not have created (*bara'*) *tohu*.

Thus, given the meaning of *bara'*, Genesis 1:2 was a necessary clause introducing the earth, man's domain—in contradistinction to the heavens, the divine domain—in a state of desolation and complete darkness under the grip of the two deadliest enemies of life on earth, the waters and the wind.[9] As will be made clear in the story of the flood and later in that of the exodus as well as in the prophetic teaching, these two

---

[6] See for instance Is 24:10; 34:10-11; Jer 4:23.

[7] *bohu* is secondary; besides Gen 1:2, it is found only in Is 34:11 and Jer 4:23, and in all three instances together with *tohu*, whereas the latter occurs frequently on its own.

[8] *tohu* in Is 40:17, 23; 41:29 44:9; 45:18, 19; 49:4; 59:4; *bara'* in Is 40:26, 28; 41:20; 42:5; 43:1, 7, 15; 45:7 (twice), 8, 12, 18 (twice); 54:16 (twice).

[9] In its way, this verse corresponds to the later "when no plant of the field was yet in the earth and no herb of the field had yet sprung up" (Gen 2:5) introducing the second creation narrative.

enemies are a necessary evil since life on earth cannot subsist without water and air. However, they are beneficial only when they are controlled by God; otherwise, if they are unleashed by him, they are destructive. This double feature, so to speak, of the winds and waters is repeatedly stressed in the biblical narratives in order to remind the hearers that life is ultimately a gift of God and not a given that is to be taken for granted, as will be made abundantly clear in the Book of Deuteronomy. My reading of the negative function of Genesis 1:2 is corroborated in that the divine actions on the first three days of creation—half of the creation period in Genesis 1!—are against darkness and the waters, to dispel the former over one day (Gen 1:3-5) and to control the latter on the second and third days (vv.6-10) in order for life to start and take hold (vv.1-13). This apparently lengthy divine battle against the "enemies" is actually functional in the story. Each of the actions on the following second triad of days corresponds to what was accomplished on the parallel day of the first triad. It is as though the first triad prepares for the second, with the clear intention to say that had God not done what he did on the first three days, the "beings" spoken of on the following three days would not have been able to subsist and find their subaltern function in God's plan for his entire creation. The sun, moon, and stars (day four) are merely there to point out to the time cycle originating with God (day one). The fish and animals of the waters and the fowl of the air (day five) live in the domains already created for them (day two). The land animals and the human beings (day six) share the same earth and vegetation provided proactively for them on day three. This "absoluteness" of God in comparison with anyone or anything else, including the deities "moon" and "sun" as well as the human being, is nothing else than the fruit of the seed already planted in the teachings of the two "fathers of scripture," Ezekiel

and Second Isaiah.[10] Just as the latter's influence can be seen in
the terminology of *bara'* and *tohu*, the "presence" of the former
is evident in that "firmament" (*raqiya'*) is a staple of Genesis 1 (9
times) and Ezekiel (1:22, 23, 25, 26; 10:1) in scripture.[11] Thus,
the "mood" of Genesis 1 is the same as that of Ezekiel 1 and,
consequently, precludes the reading of the first creation narrative
as anthropocentric, as was unfortunately done in subsequent
theology under the undue influence of Greek philosophy. Such
is corroborated by what we hear at the outset of Second Isaiah:

> A voice says, "Cry!" And I said, "What shall I cry?" All flesh is
> grass, and all its beauty is like the flower of the field. The grass
> withers, the flower fades, when the breath of the Lord blows upon
> it; surely the people is grass. The grass withers, the flower fades;
> but the word of our God will stand for ever. (Is 40:6-8)

It is then of essence to remember when hearing the first creation
narrative that its subject matter is not the human being, but
rather "the heavens and the earth" whose mention brackets the
entire passage (Gen 1:1 and 2:4). As we shall see, the human
being is just an element in this totality.

The Six Days of Creation (Gen 1:3-13)

Darkness is overcome by the light God made. Not only does
the light of day dispel the darkness of the night, but the day
becomes the time of "life," the period during which most of the
animals and the human beings function, whereas the night is the
period of the "lack of life," as it were. Moreover, the light's
"upper hand" is reflected in that the totality of night and day
comes to be known as "day," which term, in turn, becomes the

---

[10] See *OTI₁* 29-40.
[11] It occurs elsewhere only in Ps 19:2; 150:1, and Dan 12:3.

basic unit of time: notice how Genesis 1:5 ends with "one day" rather than "first day." Once the time unit is defined by the light that God made, the following units are referred to as second, third, fourth, fifth, sixth, and seventh.

Then God makes the heavens on the second day and the earth on the third day, by controlling the other opponent, the waters. It is interesting that the author relegates talking about the hosts of heavens until the fourth day, whereas he describes the rise of vegetation life on earth upon speaking of the formation of earth on the third day. The earth is described as "mother earth" producing under God's will without need for either sun or seasons, since these are not posited by God until the following day. That this is intentional is corroborated by the fact that the sun and moon are not named, but simply referred to as luminaries, lanterns hanging in the heavens just like the rest of the unnamed stars. Moreover, they are assigned as mere servants to ensure the continuity of what God has already established on day one, the separation between light and darkness (Gen 1:18). The reason is that they were powerful deities in the pantheon of Babylon, the city that became the quintessence of arrogance in scripture and, for that reason, would be brought to naught by God later in Genesis (11:1-9).

The author's handling of the fifth and sixth days is very interesting since they deal with the making of the "animal"[12] kingdom in its entirety, including the human being. The classical anthropological approach of singling out the human being and dealing with Genesis 1:26-28 as though they stood on their own, has actually distorted the intention of the scriptural

---

[12] I am taking this term in its original meaning, from the Latin *anima* which is the translation of the Hebrew *nepheš* (breath). Thus, the animal kingdom includes all creatures that breathe the way human beings do.

text. What was meant to hold human arrogance in check became a springboard to enhance it to the level of blasphemy: what is forbidden even to the deities became the fate of the mortal human being! A more thorough exegesis of the text is of import.

First and foremost, a reminder is in order here. Genesis 1-4 is not about the human being whose story (*toledot*) is the subject matter of Genesis 5:1-6:8. The first four chapters are rather the story (*toledot*) of "the heavens and the earth," that is, of God's entire creation. Unless this is kept in mind, then one is bound to mishandle the text. Secondly, the intention of Genesis is definitely not to glorify the human beings, but rather to make sure they understand they are merely "like grass and the flower of the field" (Is 40:6-8), "dust to dust" (Gen 2:7; 3:14, 19). My thesis is borne out by the following features of the text, which are literary devices on the author's part to preempt any possible "essential" uniqueness of the human being within the created realm.

On the fifth day we hear of the populating of both the waters and the heavens. The latter are part of the pair "heavens and earth" and it was already the scene of divine activity on the fourth day. However, it is what happens in the seas that is interesting, since God's intervention is targeting an inimical domain, the waters which he spent two full days, the second and the third, to subdue. In dealing with the earth on the third day, God gave it, as it were, a free hand in the production of life without his express intervention:

> And God said, "Let the earth put forth vegetation, plants yielding seed, and fruit trees bearing fruit in which is their seed, each according to its kind, upon the earth." And it was so. The earth brought forth vegetation, plants yielding seed according to their

own kinds, and trees bearing fruit in which is their seed, each according to its kind. And God saw that it was good. (Gen 1:11-12)

When it comes to the waters, however, although God allows it to produce life on its own (And God said, "Let the waters *bring forth swarms* (*yišreṣu*) of living creatures (*kol nepheš ḥayyah*) and let birds fly above the earth across the firmament of the heavens"; v.20), nevertheless he stills intervenes directly: "So God *created* (*baraʾ*) the great sea monsters (*tanninim*; dragons) and every living creature (*kol nepheš ha-ḥayyah*) that moves, with which the waters swarm (*šareṣu*), according to their kinds and every winged bird according to its kind. And God saw that it was good." (v.21) These two verses present the real turning point in preparation for the making of land animals and man on the following day.

What is noticeable is that God's intervention does not add anything to the result of his ordering the waters to produce life. Consequently, the two new features introduced by the author are intentional and thus of import: (a) God's intervention is an act of creation (*baraʾ*) which, outside its occurrence in the initial title (1:1) and the concluding statement (2:4a), is used only once more, in conjunction with the making of man (1:27); (b) besides and before the living creatures already mentioned in 1:20, God *creates* the great sea monsters (v.21). By saying that, the sea monster becomes exclusively the product, not of the waters, but of God who thus shows himself in control of the threatening waters. Indeed, the sea monster (Leviathan) functions as the personalization of the enmity of the sea waters and their power to submerge and swallow,[13] which God will overpower by

---

[13] Jer 51:34; Ezek 29:3; 32:2.

destroying it.[14] However, here we are told that God creates (*bara'*) the sea monsters, that is, heals them from their enmity, restores them, brings them back to their "sanity" by making them just another set of "living creatures" in the sea.[15] Thus *bara'* actually means to render someone functional, according to God's will, in one's given setting. Whatever power or majesty one is endowed with, one is to use it subserviently to the will of God who is the only master. This is precisely the function of *bara'* in the making of man, as we shall see. The conclusion is unmistakable: the additional two features in Genesis 1:21 (the mention of the sea monsters as well as the use of the verb *bara'*) are not introduced by happenstance but are functional within the entirety of the story of "the *toledot* of the heavens and the earth" by preparing for the creation of man as a leading figure among God's "living creatures" rather than as someone special per se.

My reading is actually corroborated in that on the sixth day God's creating activity is divided between beasts and man. At a closer look, one even finds that the "making" of man and that of the animals are closely connected. Just as the creation of the sea-living creatures prepared for that of man, so also does the making of the beasts:

> And God *made* the beasts of the earth according to their kinds and the cattle according to their kinds, and everything that creeps upon the *ground* (*'adamah*) according to its kind. And God saw that it was good. Then God said, "Let us *make man* (*'adam*) in our image, after our likeness; and let them have dominion over the fish of the sea, and over the birds of the air, and over the cattle, and

[14] Ps 74:13; Ps 148:7; Is 27:1; 51:9.
[15] Compare with Ps 104:25-27 where Leviathan was "formed"—just as Adam and the animals are in Gen 2—by God as one of the living creatures of the waters.

over all the earth, and over every creeping thing that creeps upon the earth." (Gen 1:25-26)

On the one hand, the same verb "make" is used of animals and man. On the other hand, grammatically, in Hebrew, 'adamah is the feminine of the masculine noun 'adam. By the time we encounter the term 'adam (Gen 1:26), which is specific to the human being, we have already "heard" its sound in the previous verse (v.25) in conjunction with the other animals. Thus to the hearer, the text sounds as saying that the "ground" functions as the mother of both the beasts and man. That the reference to "ground" was done intentionally in this passage can be gathered from the fact that, in the larger context (vv. 24, 27-30), the animals are repeatedly and systematically connected with the earth ('eres) and not the ground ('adamah):

And God said, "Let the *earth* bring forth living creatures according to their kinds: cattle and creeping things and beasts of the *earth* according to their kinds." And it was so... Then God said, "Let us make man in our image, after our likeness; and let them have dominion over the fish of the sea, and over the birds of the air, and over the cattle, and over all the *earth*, and over every creeping thing that creeps upon the *earth*." So God created the man in his own image, in the image of God he created him; male and female he created them. And God blessed them, and God said to them, "Be fruitful and multiply, and fill the earth and subdue it; and have dominion over the fish of the sea and over the birds of the air and over every living thing that moves upon the *earth*." And God said, "Behold, I have given you every plant yielding seed which is upon the face of all the earth, and every tree with seed in its fruit; you shall have them for food. And to every beast of the *earth*, and to every bird of the air, and to everything that creeps on the *earth*, everything that has the breath of life, I have given every green plant for food." And it was so. (vv.24, 26-30)

The latter passage (vv.26-30) is interesting in that it underscores man's dependence on the earth *as one of the earth's creatures,* thus emphasizing the priority of earth and not man in God's plan. Just as the animals were introduced as creatures of the *'adamah* (ground) before *'adam* (man) is introduced, so also are animals presented as "having the breath of life (a living breath; *nepheš hayyah)*" (v.30) just as the sea creatures earlier (vv.20-21) *before* man is formed into a living being [living breath; *nepheš hayyah*] (2:7). The priority of the earth over man in the purview of the author of the *"toledot* of the heavens and the earth" in Genesis 1-4,[16] is sealed in that later, when Adam (*'adam*) transgresses God's commandment, it is not he but the ground (*'adamah*), the source of his sustenance and life as well as origin, which is cursed:

> And to Adam he said, "Because you have listened to the voice of your wife, and have eaten of the tree of which I commanded you, 'You shall not eat of it,' cursed is the *ground* because of you; in toil you shall eat of it all the days of your life; thorns and thistles it shall bring forth to you; and you shall eat the plants of the field. In the sweat of your face you shall eat bread till you return to the *ground*, for out of it you were taken; you are dust, and to dust you shall return." (Gen 3:17-19)

The "oneness" of the animal and human realm is further evidenced in a curious feature in the description of the sixth day. Whereas both fish and fowl are blessed with a similar blessing (And God blessed them, saying, "Be fruitful and multiply and fill the waters in the seas, and let birds multiply on the earth"; 1:22) as that of man (So God created man in his own image, in the image of God he created him; male and female he created them. And God blessed them, and God said to them, "Be fruitful and

---

[16] The biblical author will deal specifically with the *toledot* of Adam in Genesis 5:1-6:8.

multiply"; vv.27-28), the land animals do not seem to have a share in such a blessing. However, since the result of the blessing is procreation that ensures the continuity of the "kinds" of beings and "God made the beasts of the earth according to their *kinds* and the cattle according to their *kinds*, and everything that creeps upon the ground according to its *kind* (v.25)," it stands to reason to conclude that the land animals were blessed by God in the same way as the fish, the fowl, and man. The omission must then be intentional and thus functional in the story. Its only plausible reason is to subsume the land animals together with the human being under the one blessing, since they procreate through the same medium, birth, just as the fish and the fowl were joined in the same blessing since their procreation follow the same medium.

The question remains, "Why weren't the land animals expressly joined with the human beings in the same blessing, as in the case of the fish and fowl?" Had the author done so, then it would have been difficult for him to make the statement regarding the human being's rule over the entire animal kingdom, including the land animals:

> So God created man in his own image, in the image of God he created him; male and female he created them. And God blessed them, and God said to them, "Be fruitful and multiply, and fill the earth and subdue it; and *have dominion over the fish of the sea and over the birds of the air and over every living thing that moves upon the earth.*" (vv.27-28)

On the other hand, had he opted for two separate blessings, then he would have jeopardized the oneness of divine creation on the sixth day, that all beings share mother earth that feeds them all in the same way, as is clear from the subsequent statement:

And God said, "Behold, I have given you every plant yielding seed which is upon the face of all the earth, and every tree with seed in its fruit; you shall have them for food. And to every beast of the earth, and to every bird of the air, and to everything that creeps on the earth, *everything that has the breath of life* (*'ašer bo nepheš ḥayyah*), I have given every green plant for food." And it was so. (vv.29-30)

The importance of this last statement, which brings together God's entire creation into total oneness under the aegis of earth, the feeding mother, can be seen in the concluding statement where reference is made to *everything* that God made: "And God saw *everything* that he had made, and behold, *it was very good*. And there was evening and there was morning, a sixth day." (v.31) Only then, after insuring that life will continue thanks to the feeding earth, are we told that "the heavens and the earth were completed, and all the host of them" (2:1).

The Making of the Human Beings

It is *within* this setting that we hear about the human beings and their subservient function in maintaining God's world in as "good" a condition as it was when he created it, nothing less and definitely nothing more.[17] One thing is sure; in presenting the human being in Genesis 1:26-28 the author is clearly using

---

[17] So-called theological anthropology, which developed under the influence of Greek—especially Platonic—philosophy, read Genesis 1:26-28 out of context as an independent unit written to describe or speak of the human being *per se*, and thus ended up distorting the initial biblical message by delving in an unhealthy and unending debate regarding the so-called personal relation between God and man, and how man is to accomplish it.

kingly (divine) terminology: image,[18] likeness,[19] and rule (have dominion) over,[20] and subdue.[21] The question becomes, "Why kingly and not fatherly terminology, especially when this is how Adam functions both at the end of the *toledot* of the heavens and the earth (Gen 4) and at the beginning of his own *toledot* (Gen 5)?" The answer lies in the basic anti-kingly stand that pervades scripture through and through. It is in Babylon, the land where God exiled Judah for the disobedience of its kings, that he raised Ezekiel the "son of man," that is, a mere human being (Ezek 1:1-3; 2:1-5), to lead his people instead of the "sons of God," that is, the kings who failed to shepherd his flock (Ezek 34). One is to remember that the divine curse against the leaders includes, besides the human beings in the latter's care, the land itself they rule with all that lives in it:

> But if you will not obey the voice of the Lord your God or be careful to do all his commandments and his statutes which I command you this day, then all these curses shall come upon you and overtake you. Cursed shall you be in the city, and cursed shall you be in the field. Cursed shall be your basket and your kneading-trough. Cursed shall be the fruit of your body, and the

---

[18] In Am 5:26 the term *ṣelem* (image) refers to the statue of a deity *as king*: "You shall take up Sakkuth your king, and Kaiwan your star-god, your images, which you made for yourselves." Thus *ṣelem* refers to the statue of either the deity (as king) or the king.

[19] The noun *demut* (likeness) and the verb *damah* (compare) are the main topic of Is 40:12-31 in conjunction with the "statues" of the deities, monarchs of their peoples. The same *damah* occurs in a passage belittling the Babylonian deities Bel and Nebo for the same reason (Is 46:1-7) and in another against Pharaoh, the earthly king *par excellence* (Ezek 31). Last but not least the noun *demut* is used profusely (10 times) in Ezek 1 to describe the "appearance" of God.

[20] The verb *radah* is used of the King of Babylon in Is 14:6 and of Egypt in Ezek 29:15, in conjunction with their "ruling over the nations." The same verb is applied to harsh rule of the kings of Israel over their people (Ezek 34:4).

[21] In 2 Sam 8:11 the verb *kabaš* is said of David's subjugation of the nations. In Jer 34:11 it describes King Hezekiah's subjugation and enslavement of his people; in v.16 the same is done with the leaders who share the king's power.

fruit of your ground, the increase of your cattle, and the young of your flock. Cursed shall you be when you come in, and cursed shall you be when you go out... You shall betroth a wife, and another man shall lie with her; you shall build a house, and you shall not dwell in it; you shall plant a vineyard, and you shall not use the fruit of it. Your ox shall be slain before your eyes, and you shall not eat of it; your ass shall be violently taken away before your face, and shall not be restored to you; your sheep shall be given to your enemies, and there shall be no one to help you... A nation which you have not known shall eat up the fruit of your ground and of all your labors; and you shall be only oppressed and crushed continually... You shall carry much seed into the field, and shall gather little in; for the locust shall consume it. You shall plant vineyards and dress them, but you shall neither drink of the wine nor gather the grapes; for the worm shall eat them. You shall have olive trees throughout all your territory, but you shall not anoint yourself with the oil; for your olives shall drop off. You shall beget sons and daughters, but they shall not be yours; for they shall go into captivity. All your trees and the fruit of your ground the locust shall possess. (Deut 28:15-19, 30-31, 33, 38-42)

Thus, the kingly terminology used to describe the human being in Genesis 1 is in view of the latter's disobedience whose result is the curse of the earth[22] and all that lives on it in Genesis 3. Genesis 1:26-28 is functional within the *toledot* of the heavens and the earth rather than a description of the intrinsic traits of the human being, as those verses were treated in classical philosophical theology. They pump up, as it were, the human being in order to invite the hearers to accept more readily the harshness of God's verdict in Genesis 3:14-19.

---

[22] The parallelism is clearer in Hebrew since both land and earth in English are the translations of the same Hebrew noun *'ereṣ*.

In view of the above, the reading of Genesis 1:26-28 becomes simple. The seriousness of the matter—assigning his representative—requires a special deliberation on the part of God. What has been taken as divine (trinitarian) plural[23] is actually the plural of deliberation.[24] It is used elsewhere both of God and of David and, in both cases, with interplay between the first person singular and the first person plural:

> And I heard the voice of the Lord saying, "Whom shall *I* send, and who will go for *us*?" (Is 6:8)[25]

> Then David said to Gad, "I am in great distress; let *us* fall into the hand of the Lord, for his mercy is great; but let *me* not fall into the hand of man." (2 Sam 24:14)

Image and likeness are the classical repetition of the same thing in ancient literature that was meant to be heard. The function of the doubling pair is merely underscoring, similar to our "the long and the short of (a story)" or "the length and the breadth (of something)." That is why in the immediately following verse the author drops likeness and sticks with image. In Genesis 5 he does the inverse: having begun with likeness (v.1), he expands it into likeness and image (v.3).[26]

In Genesis 1:27, what was introduced as the making of Adam (v.26) is presented as an act of creation (*bara'*), meaning that this

---

[23] The divine trinity, technically speaking, is New Testamental. So to read it in Genesis 1:26 is merely a retrojection and thus an *eisegesis* (reading into). For why should a plural be necessarily reflective of three, and not another plural number?

[24] It corresponds to our English phrase "consult oneself," as though there were two persons. In Arabic the plural of deliberation is part of daily language.

[25] Actually the setting of Is 6 is similar to that of Genesis 1: in either case, God is deliberating because he is about to commission his plenipotentiary representative.

[26] See below my comments on that passage.

is the way *ha'adam* (the man; the human being)[27] is supposed to be, male and female, without which condition there would be no humanity at all. Also, the shift from the singular to the plural in v.27 (So God created man in his own image, in the image of God he created *him*; male and female he created *them*) is of import, as is clear from the fact that not only in v.28 is the addressee in the plural (And God blessed them, and God said to them), but already in v.26 the human being is referred to in the plural in God's plan (Let us make *man* in our image, after our likeness; and let *them* have dominion...). Both the plural and the express mention of sexuality[28] are intentional and to be explained along the lines of the scriptural anti-kingly stance.

Functionally, the person of the monarch is, as it were, non-sexual. On the one hand, the monarch can be a king or a queen. On the other hand and more importantly, one becomes monarch not because one's father was so, but rather when one is assigned to that position by the deity itself (Ps 2:5-9; 110:1-2; Is 9:6-8). That is why the king is known as "son of God,"[29] that is, the child of one parent exclusively; he is son by God's will, not by begetting. So, by establishing that, in God's plan, the "kingly" rule over God's creation is to be and thus can be done through a "(son of) man" that is born and multiplies sexually, according to the law of animal nature, the author is eliminating the need for a "son of God." Such already prepares for Genesis 6:1-7 and beyond that for the sin of Israel when it insists on having a king

---

[27] In Hebrew the text differentiates between *ha'adam*—with the definite article—in reference to the human being in general, and *'adam* used as the proper name of an individual who is, at the same time, the prototype of every "adamic" being.

[28] Notice the "male and female" pair instead of "man and woman" as in Gen 2.

[29] Notice the parallelism between "messiah/christ (anointed)" and "son of God" in the New Testament (e.g. Mt 16:16; 26:63; Mk 1:1; 14:61; Jn 11:27; 20:31)

(1 Sam 8). In scripture there is only one valid king, the Lord God.[30] God himself will decide to choose Ezekiel to lead his people out of the land of bondage where they had ended due to their kings' misbehavior, as he had done earlier through the "(son of) man" Moses and against the will of Pharaoh the "king of Egypt" (Ex 1-14). This is indeed the will of God and the kind of rule he established to run his creation "and God saw everything that he had made, and behold, it was very good" (Gen 1:31), good the extent that there was no need for a king.[31] This is precisely the message of Genesis 1, a blow in the face to the surrounding imperial civilizations. This message will be iterated and underscored in Genesis 11:1-9 just before the appearance of Abraham, another "(son of) man" who routed four mighty kings (Gen 14).

The Seventh Day

Although the terminology used here (work [*mela'kah*]; rested [*šabat*]; hallowed) is in view of the institution of the sabbath (Ex 20:8-11; 31:12-17), the author intentionally avoids the mention of the latter as a noun (*šabbat*) out of respect for its establishment as a central facet of the Law. Furthermore, in contradistinction with Exodus where the sabbath is linked to rest and sanctification, in Deuteronomy that same day functions as a day of remembrance of the exodus from Egypt (5:12-15) which is, again, still in the future. However, what is important in this regard for my reading of what happened on the seventh day is that in both Decalogues the sabbath rest includes the land animals:

---

[30] See e.g. Is 6:5; 41:21; 43:15; 44:6; Ps *passim*.

[31] This, in turn, explains why Jesus, God's ultimate emissary, refused time and again to be hailed as a king, as the "son of God" (e.g. Mt 4:3-7; Mk 3:11-12; Jn 6:15).

Six days you shall labor, and do all your work; but the seventh day is a sabbath to the Lord your God; in it you shall not do any work, you, or your son, or your daughter, your manservant, or your maidservant, *or your cattle*, or the sojourner who is within your gates. (Ex 20:9-10)

Six days you shall labor, and do all your work; but the seventh day is a sabbath to the Lord your God; in it you shall not do any work, you, or your son, or your daughter, or your manservant, or your maidservant, *or your ox, or your ass, or any of your cattle*, or the sojourner who is within your gates, that your manservant and your maidservant may rest as well as you. (Deut 5:13-14)

Actually the rest of the seventh day has in its purview all the elements involved in the sixth day, including the earth, the mother that supports all animal life on it and needs the sabbath rest in order to fulfill its mandate, as we hear in the Law:

The Lord said to Moses on Mount Sinai, "Say to the people of Israel, 'When you come into the land which I give you, the land shall keep a sabbath to the Lord. Six years you shall sow your field, and six years you shall prune your vineyard, and gather in its fruits; but in the seventh year there shall be a sabbath of solemn rest for the land, a sabbath to the Lord; you shall not sow your field or prune your vineyard. What grows of itself in your harvest you shall not reap, and the grapes of your undressed vine you shall not gather; it shall be a year of solemn rest for the land. *The sabbath of the land shall provide food for you, for yourself and for your male and female slaves and for your hired servant and the sojourner who lives with you; for your cattle also and for the beasts that are in your land all its yield shall be for food.'*" (Lev 25:1-7)

The intimate link between the sabbatical year and the sabbath is at its clearest in the following passage:

For six years you shall sow your land and gather in its yield; but
the seventh year you shall let it rest and lie fallow, that the poor of
your people may eat; *and what they leave the wild beasts may eat.*
You shall do likewise with your vineyard, and with your olive
orchard. Six days you shall do your work, but on the seventh day
you shall rest; *that your ox and your ass may have rest*, and the son
of your bondmaid, and the alien, may be refreshed. (Ex 23:10-12)

I still believe that, in dealing with the seventh day in the way
he did (Gen 2:1-3), the author had something else in mind that
would be functional in the second creation narrative that is
introduced in the immediately following verse 4, which also
functions as the hinge between the two creation narratives.[32]
Otherwise, since the subject matter of both narratives is not
God, but the heavens and the earth he created or made (Gen 1:1;
2:4), the information concerning the seventh day is left
"hanging," with no need for it. Indeed, Genesis 1:31-2:1 would
have been a most fitting ending to the first narrative: "And God
saw everything that he had made, and behold, it was very good.
And there was evening and there was morning, a sixth day. Thus
the heavens and the earth were finished, and all the host of
them." On the other hand, it is the verb *nuaḥ* (rest) that is used
in the Decalogue to describe God's rest in a text that, otherwise,
repeats verbatim Genesis 2:3 "… for in six days the Lord made
heaven and earth, the sea, and all that is in them, and *rested* the
seventh day; therefore the Lord blessed the *sabbath* day and
hallowed it." (Ex 20:11). Moreover, in the Deuteronomic
Decalogue, it is that same verb *nuaḥ* which also bespeaks the
sabbatical rest of the human beings: "… but the seventh day is a
sabbath to the Lord your God; in it you shall not do any work,
you, or your son, or your daughter, or your manservant, or your
maidservant, or your ox, or your ass, or any of your cattle, or the

---

[32] See my comments earlier in my discussion of Gen 1:1.

sojourner who is within your gates, that your manservant and your maidservant may *rest* as well as you." (Deut 5:14)[33] Consequently, the author did not have simply in mind the (sabbatical) rest per se, but also the sabbath itself and what it entails.

In many an instance and in different books, mention is made of the sabbath in conjunction with God's commandments, without anything to warrant such a link between the two. The first instance is impressive since, for no apparent reason and without any introduction, the sabbath is mentioned at the closing of God's handing down his commandments to Moses:

> Say to the people of Israel, "You shall keep my sabbaths, for this is a sign between me and you throughout your generations, that you may know that I, the Lord, sanctify you. You shall keep the sabbath, because it is holy for you; every one who profanes it shall be put to death; whoever does any work on it, that soul shall be cut off from among his people. Six days shall work be done, but the seventh day is a sabbath of solemn rest, holy to the Lord; whoever does any work on the sabbath day shall be put to death. Therefore the people of Israel shall keep the sabbath, observing the sabbath throughout their generations, as a perpetual covenant. It is a sign for ever between me and the people of Israel that in six days the Lord made heaven and earth, and on the seventh day he rested, and was refreshed." (Ex 31:13-17)

The same is done at the end of the interlude of Israel's blasphemy with the golden calf that forces Moses to renew the covenant (Ex 32-34). At his descent from the

---

[33] If anything, it is the earth that rests (*šabat*) on the sabbatical year (Lev 25:2), which in turn corroborates my reading that the subject matter in the first creation narrative is not the human being, but rather the earth (and the heavens).

mountain with the new set of tablets (34:29-35), we immediately hear the following:

> Moses assembled all the congregation of the people of Israel, and said to them, "These are the things which the Lord has commanded you to do. Six days shall work be done, but on the seventh day you shall have a holy sabbath of solemn rest to the Lord; whoever does any work on it shall be put to death; you shall kindle no fire in all your habitations on the sabbath day." (Ex 35:1-3)

This feature becomes axial in Ezekiel's rendering of the wilderness journey:

> So I led them out of the land of Egypt and brought them into the wilderness. I gave them my statutes and showed them my ordinances, by whose observance man shall live. Moreover I gave them my sabbaths, as a sign between me and them, that they might know that I the Lord sanctify them. But the house of Israel rebelled against me in the wilderness; they did not walk in my statutes but rejected my ordinances, by whose observance man shall live; and my sabbaths they greatly profaned. Then I thought I would pour out my wrath upon them in the wilderness, to make a full end of them. But I acted for the sake of my name, that it should not be profaned in the sight of the nations, in whose sight I had brought them out. Moreover I swore to them in the wilderness that I would not bring them into the land which I had given them, a land flowing with milk and honey, the most glorious of all lands, because they rejected my ordinances and did not walk in my statutes, and profaned my sabbaths; for their heart went after their idols. Nevertheless my eye spared them, and I did not destroy them or make a full end of them in the wilderness. And I said to their children in the wilderness, do not walk in the statutes of your fathers, nor observe their ordinances, nor defile yourselves with their idols. I the Lord am your God; walk in my statutes, and be careful to observe my ordinances, and hallow my sabbaths that

they may be a sign between me and you, that you may know that I the Lord am your God. But the children rebelled against me; they did not walk in my statutes, and were not careful to observe my ordinances, by whose observance man shall live; they profaned my sabbaths. Then I thought I would pour out my wrath upon them and spend my anger against them in the wilderness. But I withheld my hand, and acted for the sake of my name, that it should not be profaned in the sight of the nations, in whose sight I had brought them out. Moreover I swore to them in the wilderness that I would scatter them among the nations and disperse them through the countries, because they had not executed my ordinances, but had rejected my statutes and profaned my sabbaths, and their eyes were set on their fathers' idols. (Ezek 20:10-24)[34]

Finally, in Nehemiah, we have a reminiscence of what we hear in Deuteronomy:

Thou didst come down upon Mount Sinai, and speak with them from heaven and give them right ordinances and true laws, good statutes and commandments, and thou didst make known to them thy holy sabbath and command them commandments and statutes and a law by Moses thy servant. (Neh 9:13-14)

Thus, we have in all three parts of the Old Testament scripture, the Law, the Prophets, and the Writings, a linking between the sabbath and the issuance of God's commandments. This is precisely what we find in the New Testament regarding the hearing of scripture on the sabbaths.[35]

Consequently, the sabbath rest is not only a *terminus ad quem* but also the start of a period that puts God's hearers to the test as to whether they will abide by his commandments and live, or

---

[34] See also Ezek 22:26; 44:24.
[35] See e.g. Lk 4:16-21; Acts 13:14-15, 44; 15:21.

not. And this is precisely how Genesis 2:1-3 function. As a description of the seventh day, those verses look backwards by summing up God's work as securing the provision needed to sustain the world (Gen 1:29-30), which parallels what one hears next in Nehemiah: "Thou didst give them bread from heaven for their hunger and bring forth water for them from the rock for their thirst, and thou didst tell them to go in to inherit the land (earth) which thou hadst sworn to give them." (9:15) At the same time, they prepare for the second creation narrative where the first verbal contact between God and the man (*ha'adam*) is a commandment unto life so long as man abided by it:

> And the Lord God commanded the man, saying, "You may freely eat of every tree of the garden; but of the tree of the knowledge of good and evil you shall not eat, for in the day that you eat of it you shall die." (Gen 2:16-17)

The element life is deftly encoded in the terminology describing the seventh day in that God "blessed" it (v.3), which verb was previously used in conjunction with living beings and referred to the ensuring of their continued life on God's earth through procreation. I suggest, then, that it is the entire passage Genesis 2:1-4—and not simply 2:4—that functions as a hinge between the two creation narratives, both summing up the preceding and setting up the scene for the following. It is saying to the hearer: Now that God has put everything into place on earth and completed *his* work which he found to be "very good," let us see whether the man, assigned as his plenipotentiary representative, will behave to maintain God's will in and for the world he created. It is only God who rested on the seventh day; the man has not yet done (made)[36] anything. His turn is about to

---

[36] In Hebrew it is the same verb *'asah* used to speak of God's creative activity in Gen 1:1-2:4, which means both "make" and "do." Notice how RSV translates that same

begin. Without Genesis 2:1-4, which I showed to be technically speaking unnecessary as an ending to Genesis 1, the two creation narratives would have remained parallel and not interconnected.

Eden

Since the second creation narrative narrows its interest to one individual as exemplar for the rest of humanity,[37] the domain changes from the earth to a garden as representative of the earth. This is clear from two facts. On the one hand, the garden and its produce are the workmanship of God in the same way as the earth was in Genesis 1: "And the Lord God planted a garden in Eden, in the east; and there he put the man whom he had formed. And out of the ground the Lord God made to grow every tree that is pleasant to the sight and good for food, the tree of life also in the midst of the garden, and the tree of the knowledge of good and evil." (Gen 2:8-9) On the other hand, although the man was put in the garden, he was to till the *earth* (of that garden): "The Lord God took the man and put him in the garden of Eden to till it (the earth) and keep it (the earth)." (v.15) The English translation does not capture the original Hebrew since the pronoun "it" sounds as referring to the garden. But in Hebrew, the noun *gan* (garden) is masculine whereas the noun *'ereṣ* (earth) is feminine, and the pronoun after each of "till" and "keep" is the feminine "her." Furthermore, the Hebrew clearly reflects the fact that the fruits of the garden remain God's work as in v.9. Whereas the English has "put the man (him)" in both cases (Gen 2:8 and 15), the Hebrew of v.15 reads

---

verb twice as "had done" in Gen 1:2-3, which was rendered systematically as "made" in Gen 1:7, 16, 25, 31 and "had made" in Gen 24.
[37] Notice the consistent use of *ha'adam* (the man) in Genesis 2-3.

yannihehu (and he made him enjoy his stay).[38] The pain of working the earth of the garden will come later as a punishment, as we shall see.

Often, due to our egotistically anthropocentric approach to scripture, many of us view, if not already the first narrative, most definitely the second one as being about the creation or formation of man. The corollary is that one starts fishing for verses concerning the human being and loses sight of the story line or thread. At the risk of iteration, the *toledot* or story of the human being does not start until Genesis 5:1. Until then we are still in the realm of the *toledot* of the heavens and the earth. The centrality of the latter in Genesis 2 and 3 is evident from the lion's share it controls in these two chapters. Suffice it to point out for the time being that the "ground" (*'adamah*) forms an *inclusio* that brackets the so-called story of Adam in Eden (Gen 2:5 and 3:24). The overall feeling is that *'adam*, the "son" of the *'adamah*, due to his disobedience to the God who made the ground and formed Adam out of it, ended up by being exiled out of the ground that bore him. Put otherwise, those two chapters are to be viewed as the story of the garden or ground of Eden rather than that of Adam in Eden. It is the story of the disaster that befell Adam's ground whose blueprint is the story of the disaster that befell the kingdoms of Israel and Judah. In both cases, curse and exile were the price of disobedience of the leader(s).

As in the case of the first narrative, it is water that is to be harnessed if there is to be life on earth, and it is only God who is in control of the matter. However, whereas the story of the flood will show the negative effect of uncontrolled water, Genesis 2

---

[38] It is the same verb whence comes the name Noah. See below on this matter.

underscores its positive effect as well as its necessity. Without water, the interrelationship of life between the *'adamah* and the *'adam* would have been impossible: no vegetation to feed man and no man to till the ground since the former is the produce of the watered earth and the latter is made out of clay, a moist ground:

> When no plant of the field was yet in the earth and no herb of the field had yet sprung up -- for the Lord God had not caused it to rain upon the earth, and there was no man to till the ground; but a mist went up from the earth and watered the whole face of the ground, then the Lord God formed (*yaṣar*, mold out of clay) man of dust from the ground, and breathed into his nostrils the breath of life (*nišmat ḥayyim*); and man became a living being (*nepheš ḥayyah*). (Gen 2:5-7)

Even the garden that God planted and filled with all kinds of trees, in which he put the man he had formed (v.8), was watered by a river. Here, in a remarkable passage (vv.10-14), the author describes the garden as a mini-world, since the river that flows out of it is the source of the four universal rivers that supported mighty kingdoms.[39] What applies to the man in the garden applies to every "living being." And the man enjoyed his life (*nuaḥ*) by tilling the earth of the garden that God granted to him (v.15).

Before leaving the passage dealing with the formation of man, I would like to point out a feature that further corroborates my understanding that the two creation narratives are closely

---

[39] Two of the rivers are the Tigris and the Euphrates. The other two have metaphorical names reflecting "gushing (of waters)" and thus mighty rivers. At any rate, they are connected with two major biblical areas known for their richness (Havilah) and power (Cush).

interconnected. In the first narrative the mighty wind and the waters were presented as a pair: "… and the spirit (*ruaḥ*; mighty wind) of God was moving over the face of the waters" (Gen 1:2) threatening to engulf anything under their waves. However, as Ezekiel teaches, the judging and punishing divine *ruaḥ*[40] can become, at God's will, a smooth breath (*nešamah*; breeze) that gathers instead of scatters, that enlivens instead of destroys (Ezek 17:1-15). This is precisely what Genesis 2:7 is playing on namely, God uses his breath, which is potentially deadly, to grant life. The destructive facet of both divine spirit and divine breath can be seen in the following passages:

> The Lord thundered from heaven, and the Most High uttered his voice. And he sent out arrows, and scattered them; lightning, and routed them. Then the channels of the sea were seen, the foundations of the world were laid bare, at the rebuke of the Lord, at the blast of the breath of his nostrils. (2 Sam 22:14-16)

> By the breath of God they perish, and by the blast of his anger they are consumed. (Job 4:9)

> In my distress I called upon the Lord; to my God I cried for help. From his temple he heard my voice, and my cry to him reached his ears. Then the earth reeled and rocked; the foundations also of the mountains trembled and quaked, because he was angry. Smoke went up from his nostrils, and devouring fire from his mouth; glowing coals flamed forth from him. (Ps 18:6-8)

> For a burning place has long been prepared; yea, for the king it is made ready, its pyre made deep and wide, with fire and wood in

---

[40] See e.g. Mt 3:11-12/Lk 3:16-17: "I baptize you with water for repentance, but he who is coming after me is mightier than I, whose sandals I am not worthy to carry; he will baptize you with the Holy Spirit and with fire. His winnowing fork is in his hand, and he will clear his threshing floor and gather his wheat into the granary, but the chaff he will burn with unquenchable fire."

abundance; the breath of the Lord, like a stream of brimstone, kindles it. (Is 30:33)

And the man will soon learn that God can shorten the life span of man by taking away the breath granted to him, as we hear at the psalmist's hand:

> O Lord, how manifold are thy works! In wisdom hast thou made them all; the earth is full of thy creatures. Yonder is the sea, great and wide, which teems with things innumerable, living things both small and great. There go the ships, and Leviathan which thou didst form to sport in it. These all look to thee, to give them their food in due season. When thou givest to them, they gather it up; when thou openest thy hand, they are filled with good things. When thou hidest thy face, they are dismayed; when thou takest away their breath, they die and return to their dust. When thou sendest forth thy Spirit, they are created; and thou renewest the face of the ground. (Ps 104:24-30)

Among the trees that God made grow in the garden were two trees that would be functional in the narrative, the tree of life and the tree of the knowledge of good and evil (Gen 2:9). In languages "pairs," whether complementary such as "heaven and earth," "men and women," "adults and children," "humans and animals," "fauna and flora" or opposite such as "black and white," "light and darkness," "day and night," "rich and poor," "big and small," are intended to speak of the totality rather than the two mentioned elements each independently. Thus the phrase "good and evil" is not to be taken as a combination of two independent elements, but as reflective of the idea of "everything." Consequently, "the knowledge of good and evil" means the knowledge of everything, which would have allowed the human being to make decisions and behave independently from God's input. Still, the choice of the pair "good and evil" over any other "pair" is interesting in this regard since discerning between good and evil is the domain of the judge. The author wanted to stress the point that God alone is not only the one that has the fullness of knowledge, but more specifically that he is the sole judge that emits the Law and judges by it, which is a scriptural staple. As plenipotentiary representative of God, man is to rule justly over God's world, yet he always remains under divine judgment. That is why the divine decision regarding the tree of the knowledge of good and evil is issued to man as a commandment, that is, as an expression of God's law that the man is accountable for (2:16-17). The result of abiding by this commandment ensures continuity of life to man, whereas the penalty of transgression is the verdict of death, as in Deuteronomy. That is to say, it is God's law and not the fruit of the earth that grants length of life as we shall hear later in Deuteronomy:

> All the commandment which I command you this day you shall be careful to do, *that you may live and multiply,* and go in and inherit the earth which the Lord swore to give to your fathers. And you shall remember all the way which the Lord your God has led you these forty years in the wilderness, that he might humble you, testing you to know what was in your heart, whether you would keep his commandments, or not. And he humbled you and let you hunger and fed you with manna, which you did not know, nor did your fathers know; that he might make you know that *man (ha'adam) does not live by bread alone, but that man (ha'adam) lives by everything that proceeds out of the mouth of the Lord.* (Deut 8:1-3)

> And if you obey the voice of the Lord your God, being careful to do all his commandments which I command you this day, the Lord your God will set you high above all the nations of the earth. And all these blessings shall come upon you and overtake you, if you obey the voice of the Lord your God... But if you will not

obey the voice of the Lord your God or be careful to do all his commandments and his statutes which I command you this day, then all these curses shall come upon you and overtake you. (Deut 28:1-2, 15)

The fact that man was not forbidden to eat from the tree of life meant that he was eating of it before he contravened God's command to abstain from eating from the tree of knowledge. It is important to remember this point in order to avoid the erroneous teaching held by many that, had he not transgressed, man would have lived eternally on earth. In Genesis 3:19, it is not death that is instated, but rather the difficulty of life. Death is assumed as a given: "In the sweat of your face you shall eat bread *till you return to the ground, for* out of it you were taken; *for* you are dust, and to dust you shall return." I shall deal with the statement of the prohibition of eating from the tree of life in its own time.

The Building of Woman

This section of the story is craftily construed to show that very early the man was asserting his independence from God, which will lead to his mishandling the authority given him over the rest of creation. He will end up as a tyrant rather than as a caretaker: "To the woman he [the Lord God] said, 'I will greatly multiply your pain in childbearing; in pain you shall bring forth children, yet your desire shall be for your husband, and he shall rule (*mašal*) over you.'" (Gen 3:16) The desire versus rule pair, which occurs only one more time in the Bible to describe Cain's struggle with sin (sin is couching at the door; its desire is for you, but you must master [*mašal*] it; 4:7) clearly refers to a relation of tension where each party is trying to overcome the other's hold.

In order to set up for the disastrous ending, the story begins with God's intention to find a companion for the man who would help him in his daily life, an *'ezer* (helper). However this *'ezer* is qualified with the preposition *neged* which means both "facing" and "opposite." Put otherwise, the intended "face to face" companionship had the potential of becoming an opposing factor, and the outcome would depend on the man's attitude toward God's endeavor. Man found unsatisfactory all the beings formed (out of clay) by the Lord God out of the ground (*min ha'adamah,*), as was the man himself. It is as though the man was displeased with God's creation and found it to be "not good." Worse, he actually refused all that was "adamic" (out of the ground) as he was, after God's will, which thus would have been a perfect helper for him. He opted for a being that would be "built[41] out of the man (*min ha'adam*)," a being that would be man's own creation, as it were. The verb "build" (*banah*) will be used later to speak of building Nineveh and Babel (Gen 10:11; 11:5), the cities that will eventually oppress the kingdoms of Israel and Judah, and take their citizens into exile. This is precisely how Adam will end, exiled out of Eden, his ground, because he wanted to build his own "city."[42] The walled and gated city in the Ancient Near East was viewed as a mother holding her children in her bosom and, consequently, as the wife of the monarch or the deity.[43]

---

[41] RSV has "and the rib which the Lord God had taken *from* the man he made into a woman" where the original Hebrew reads "and the rib which the Lord God had taken *out of* the man he made into a woman" (Gen 2:22)

[42] The reason behind choosing a rib is that it is a bone found in quantity in the human body. One should not stretch the text's intent by saying, for instance, that the rib was selected because it is a bone that is close to the man's heart.

[43] See, e.g. Is 54:5-6: "For your Maker is your husband, the Lord of hosts is his name; and the Holy One of Israel is your Redeemer, the God of the whole earth he is called.

As for God's giving in to the wish of the man should not befuddle us since this is how God will behave when the people force the hand of Samuel to request a king against God's will (1 Sam 8):

> But the people refused to listen to the voice of Samuel; and they said, "No! But we will have a king over us, that we also may be like all the nations, and that our king may govern us and go out before us and fight our battles." And when Samuel had heard all the words of the people, he repeated them in the ears of the Lord. And the Lord said to Samuel, "*Hearken to their voice, and make them a king.*" (vv.19-22)

The intention in Samuel is to eventually show the people the result of their mistake. And this is precisely what is taking place in Genesis 2. The man ends up falling in the trap he created for himself. The kings of Israel and Judah will fall together with Samaria and Jerusalem, the cities they "built" to "help" them in their time of need.[44] Similarly, the man's own "creation," the woman who is "bone of his bones and flesh of his flesh" will drag him into "exile." One does not need to wait for the end of Genesis 3. Metaphorically this is already happening: while it is traditionally the bride who moves in to the groom's house and chambers, forgetting "her people and her father's house" (Ps

---

For the Lord has called you like a wife forsaken and grieved in spirit, like a wife of youth when she is cast off, says your God."

[44] The case of Samaria is forceful since its name in Hebrew is *šomeron* from the root *šamar* meaning "keep, protect." Moreover, King Omri is said to have built Samaria as a fort: "He bought the hill of Samaria from Shemer for two talents of silver; and he fortified the hill, and called the name of the city which he built, Samaria, after the name of Shemer, the owner of the hill." (1 Kg 16:24)

45:10),[45] here it is the man that ends up leaving his kin. Actually the text is very harshly ironical:

> Then the man said, "This at last is bone of my bones and flesh of my flesh; she shall be called Woman, because she was taken out of Man." *Therefore* a man leaves his father and his mother and cleaves to his wife, and they become one flesh. (Gen 2:23-24)

The conclusion is a non sequitur. If the first formed human being (*ha'adam*) is now the "man" (*'iš*; the male human being) who defines the "woman" (*'iššah*; the female human being),[46] then one would expect that she would be under his aegis, and not vice-versa. The irony is evident. Man's arrogance is in wanting to chip in his own blueprint in the formation of his counterpart. Instead of a counterpart who would help him enjoy life (*nuah*) in the garden, he ends up with a partner whose beguiling by the serpent will trigger a chain of events leading to man's exile out of the garden! As any tyrant, the man reaps what he has sown: woman went her way, not God's way, just as the man did. They both contravened God's will by pushing for their own and thus proved not to be fit to live in *God's* garden.

The last comment in the section of the building of woman is a statement that bridges this section and the following one which will describe that chain of events: "And the man and his wife were both naked (*'arummim*; the plural of *'arom*), and were not ashamed." (Gen 2:25) In scripture shame related to nakedness has nothing to do with sexuality; it is rather the shame of being belittled, as is "put to shame," and as such it is a punishment by God:

---

[45] See also the stories of Rebekah in Gen 24 and the Shulammite in the Song of Songs.
[46] Just as in English we can hear the wordplay between "man" and "woman" so also there is an assonance in Hebrew between the original masculine noun *'iš* and its derivative the feminine noun *'iššah*.

At that time the Lord had spoken by Isaiah the son of Amoz, saying, "Go, and loose the sackcloth from your loins and take off your shoes from your feet," and he had done so, walking naked and barefoot—the Lord said, "As my servant Isaiah has walked naked and barefoot for three years as a sign and a portent against Egypt and Ethiopia, so shall the king of Assyria lead away the Egyptians captives and the Ethiopians exiles, both the young and the old, naked and barefoot, with buttocks uncovered, to the shame of Egypt. Then they shall be dismayed and confounded because of Ethiopia their hope and of Egypt their boast." (Is 20:2-5)

Come down and sit in the dust, O virgin daughter of Babylon; sit on the ground without a throne, O daughter of the Chaldeans! For you shall no more be called tender and delicate. Take the millstones and grind meal, put off your veil, strip off your robe, uncover your legs, pass through the rivers. Your nakedness shall be uncovered, and your shame shall be seen. I will take vengeance, and I will spare no man. (Is 47:1-3)

I will scatter you like chaff driven by the wind from the desert. This is your lot, the portion I have measured out to you, says the Lord, because you have forgotten me and trusted in lies. I myself will lift up your skirts over your face, and your shame will be seen. (Jer 13:24-26)

Thus says the Lord God, Because your shame was laid bare and your nakedness uncovered in your harlotries with your lovers, and because of all your idols, and because of the blood of your children that you gave to them, therefore, behold, I will gather all your lovers, with whom you took pleasure, all those you loved and all those you loathed; I will gather them against you from every side, and will uncover your nakedness to them, that they may see all your nakedness. (Ezek 16:36-37)

"Behold, I will press you down in your place, as a cart full of sheaves presses down. Flight shall perish from the swift, and the

strong shall not retain his strength, nor shall the mighty save his
life; he who handles the bow shall not stand, and he who is swift
of foot shall not save himself, nor shall he who rides the horse save
his life; and he who is stout of heart among the mighty shall flee
away naked in that day," says the Lord. (Am 2:13-16)

It is then only when God punishes, or at least when the culprit
realizes that his action is liable to incur God's punishment, that
shame is "revealed." This is what is going to happen in Genesis
3:7. However, it is the cunningness of the serpent, who is
introduced as 'arum (cunning; 3:1), that will unveil to Adam and
the woman that they are 'erummim (naked; 3:7) or that either of
them is 'arom. The wordplay with assonance is unmistakable,
especially when one considers that the ultimate result is that the
serpent will be declared as 'arur (cursed; 3:14) and the 'adamah
(ground) as 'arurah (cursed; 3:17) by the Lord God.
Consequently, Genesis 2:25 functions as a preamble to ch.3 in
its entirety.

The Disobedience and Its Consequence

The cunning serpent uses the woman, "creation" of the man,
to get him to contravene God's express commandment. Just as
Samaria and Jerusalem are cajoled by Nineveh and Babylon away
from their "husband," the Lord (Ezek 16 and 23), so also here
the woman is cajoled by the serpent away from the man and,
ultimately, away from the Lord God. The serpent, nahaš in
Hebrew, is from a root connected with augury, which is strictly
forbidden because it leads to blasphemy against the Lord and his
authority:

You shall not practice augury (tenahašu) or witchcraft. (Lev 19:26)

There shall not be found among you any one who burns his son or
his daughter as an offering, anyone who practices divination, a

soothsayer, or an augur (*menaḥeš*), or a sorcerer, or a charmer, or a medium, or a wizard, or a necromancer. (Deut 18:10-11)

And they burned their sons and their daughters as offerings, and used divination and sorcery, and sold themselves to do evil in the sight of the Lord, provoking him to anger. (2 Kg 17:17)

And he burned his son as an offering, and practiced soothsaying and augury, and dealt with mediums and with wizards. He did much evil in the sight of the Lord, provoking him to anger. (2 Kg 21:6)

Thus, it is as though the woman was consulting with a source that would bring about God's ire, and this is precisely what happened. It is only when both the man and the woman contravened the Lord God's express order that they realized they were naked, meaning that they were put to shame (Gen 3:7). And this is done in a lawsuit style of questioning by the judge who alone fully "knows the good and the evil" (vv.8-13).

The verdict of the divine court is dreadful. The "magician" who beguiled the woman and, through her, the man is the first to be committed to the curse (vv.14-15). Just as death of which scripture speaks is the result of disobedience by divine verdict, so also is the curse, which is presented as the divine verdict for contravention of God's commandments and statutes (Deut 28:15-19). On should not imagine that before the punishment was issued the serpent looked or behaved differently. Rather, the curse lies in the continual enmity between it and the woman and, more specifically, between its seed and that of the woman, that is, the human beings in general.[47] From the metaphorical

---

[47] The term *zera'* (seed) is a generic singular meaning "progeny." RSV translates it incorrectly as "he" only because *zera'* is grammatically masculine and Hebrew has only two grammatical genders, masculine and feminine.

phraseology used (he [it] shall bruise your head, and you shall bruise his [its] heel: v.15), the threat works in favor of the human being who will present a threat to the head of the serpent, and thus total annihilation, while the serpent will hurt the heel of man, and thus harm him only marginally.

The reference to "seed," otherwise unwarranted, is to be explained by the fact that the woman is not cursed in v.16. The reason lies in that curse is the opposite of blessing (Deut 28:1-8 and 28:15-19) and blessing is expressed through procreation in Genesis 1. The punishment of woman, who will soon be called, while still in Eden, "Eve (*hawwah*)," the reason being that "she was the mother of all living (*kol hay*)" (Gen 3:20), will entail (merely) difficulty *in child bearing*. This is obviously in view of the penalty of exile, which is the death of a city in scripture. The punishment addressed to the man parallels that to the woman in the sense that it is mother earth that is cursed: desolation of a land around the city and death of its inhabitants go hand in hand with the exile of its inhabitants. The former is reflected in the difficulty of procuring food (Gen 3:17b-19a) and the latter in the death of the man and his return to dust.[48]

The laconic v. 21 (And the Lord God made for Adam and for his wife garments of skins, and clothed them) sounds as though it is standing in mid-air. In reality, its function is to underscore the mess in which man's disobedience has thrown the entire realm of creation. In order to provide animal skin or hide, one has to have slaughtered an animal. In so doing, the Lord God was showing the man and his wife the ultimate cost of the disobedience: the shame of their nakedness cannot be hid with a

---

[48] "Return to dust" smells more of a punishment in comparison to "return to the *'adamah*" for *'adam*. It is reminiscent of the punishment of the serpent that has to "eat the dust all the days of [its] life" (Gen 3:14) until it returns to it.

cloth, but with an animal sacrifice for atonement. Someone else, that is, an animal made from the same *'adamah* as *'adam* and was supposed to share that *'adamah* with man, had to be sacrificed for man's misbehavior. Again, as in Gen 2:21-22 and 1 Samuel 8, God's hand is, as it were, forced in order for him to unveil to man the gravity of his action. This decision of God will be consummated later in the following edict:

> The fear of you and the dread of you shall be upon every beast of the earth, and upon every bird of the air, upon everything that creeps on the ground and all the fish of the sea; into your hand they are delivered. Every moving thing that lives shall be food for you; and as I gave you the green plants, I give you everything. Only you shall not eat flesh with its life, that is, its blood. (Gen 9:2-4)

On the other hand, clothing is an indication of civilization, the reflection of the life of the city, which city is viewed negatively in scripture. Ultimately, God will show his true face in Ezekiel 48, as a shepherd who cares for his own in the open pasture without need for a city that provides only a transient and thus false security. The true city is rather the presence of the Lord in the midst of his own: "And the name of the city henceforth shall be, The Lord is there." (Ezek 48:35).

The statement in Genesis 3:22 (Then the Lord God said, "Behold, the man has become like one of us, knowing good and evil") means that, by becoming someone who knows good and evil, the man accedes to the divine council. However, unlike Isaiah who became a representative of the divine council by invitation (Is 6:8) and thus after having been cleansed of his sin (v.7), the man did so forcibly. Actually, it is by committing the sin of disobedience that he became a member of the divine council, or so he imagined. So, in order to give him a wake-up call, the Lord God forbids him to eat from the tree of life (Gen 3:22), the way to which will be heavily guarded with a sword of consuming fire, as a reminder that he cannot live forever as deities do. The man is dust to dust and remains so. To survive he will have to keep "tilling the ground from which he was taken," but this time "outside the garden of Eden" (v.23). This work will be done "in the sweat of [his] face" (v.19), fighting thorns and thistles (v.18), and not with enjoyment as it was originally (2:15). Consequently, eating the fruit of the tree of life would not have saved man from God's verdict when he disobeyed God's commandment, nor would grant him "life unto eternity." The "life" from this tree does not refer to eternal life; rather it refers to length of days on earth granted forever under God's aegis. Actually, God's verdict imposed the *ceasing* of eating of the fruit of the tree of life, and this divine verdict shortened man's sojourn in the garden.[49] Yet God granted the man to continue to "live" outside the garden. And, as we shall see, this same divine verdict that shortened the sojourn of man in the garden will shorten the life of the children of Jacob in the earth God grants to them whenever they contravene His commandments.

Cain and Abel

Just as the divine punishment takes away from Adam the "relaxation" in living without taking away his life, so also the same punishment takes away from woman the "relaxation" in birth-giving without taking away procreation itself. This allows

---

[49] Compare, for instance, the divine commandment "Honor your father and your mother, that your days may be long in the land which the Lord your God gives you" (Ex 20:12) with the divine verdicts "Whoever strikes his father or his mother shall be put to death" (21:15) and "Whoever curses his father or his mother shall be put to death" (21:17).

God's original blessing to continue in spite of man's sin. The intention on the part of the author to show that life as created by God will continue is made clear in the phrasing of the immediate following text that links Adam and the woman, on the one hand, with the following human generation represented by Cain, on the other hand:

> Therefore the Lord God sent him forth from the garden of Eden, to work the ground from which he was taken. He drove out the man; and at the east of the garden of Eden he placed the cherubim, and a flaming sword which turned every way, to guard the way to the tree of life. Now Adam knew Eve his wife, and she conceived and bore Cain, saying, "I have acquired a man with the Lord." And again, she bore his brother Abel. Now Abel was a keeper of sheep, and Cain a worker of the ground. (3:23-4:2)

Notice that Adam himself is granted to work outside the garden and Cain continues this mission of working the ground, which was the duty assigned to Adam in the garden.[50] More importantly, however, Cain is "acquired"[51] by Eve "with the Lord," meaning that he is acquired with God's will and blessing.

Just as the man was tested, so is his progeny now. Cain, the worker of the ground, the "earth man," was to understand that he is not its owner. If the command of the real owner, God, is that the fruit of the earth is to be shared with the earth animals and even the birds of the air (1:29-30), then the more so is it to be shared with the other human beings even if their main line of work did not entail tilling the ground and thus providing food. As shepherd, Abel's lot is to care for the sheep that provide milk

---

[50] This shows that the punishment of Adam reflects a change in condition rather than a geographical relocation.
[51] Both "Cain" and "acquire" are from the same root in Hebrew.

and wool for Cain and his like. But Cain, like his progenitor, thought that he had entitlement over every life on the earth he was working. And so he sentenced a human being to death, an action reserved solely to the judge. That is why he was brought to justice (Gen 4:6-15) as his father was before him (3:9-13).

The story is written in a way that enhances the gravity of Cain's sin:

1. Abel had nothing to do with God's decision in having had regard for Abel's offering and not for Cain's (vv.4-5). It was merely God's good pleasure in order to test Cain as he tested Adam.

2. The fairness of the test, as was the case with Adam, can be seen in that God forewarned Cain of sin that was "couching at the door"[52] and that he had to master, rule over (*mašal*) the propensity toward uncontrolled ire as a ruler should (vv.6-7). Moreover, the eventual action Cain was contemplating was expressly branded as *ḥaṭṭa't* (sin; overstepping one's boundary; v.7).

3. The swiftness with which Cain is said to have engaged in fratricide is striking. After the lengthy divine warning by God (vv.6-7) we are told: "Cain said to Abel his brother, and when they were in the field, Cain rose up against his brother Abel, and killed him." The addition "Let us go out to the field" after "brother," albeit logical, is not

---

[52] In the original Hebrew we have "the door (opening) of sin" that is the subject of "couching" and "the desire for Cain." Sin in Hebrew is a feminine noun whereas the participle "couching" and the adjectival pronoun "its" linked to "desire" are in the masculine just as "door" is. The description is of sin opening its mouth to engulf Cain, most probably in view of the ground that will open its mouth to receive and engulf Abel's shed blood (Gen 4:11).

found in the original Hebrew. The author intended to underscore Cain's rashness, a trait unworthy of a "master" who is supposed to rule with wisdom.

4. Abel, as his name in Hebrew *hebel* (breath, vanity)[53] indicates, is representative of any plain being whose life is just a passing moment, "from dust to dust" and "like the withering grass or the fading flower of the field" (Is 40:6-7). The insignificance of Abel is further brought in relief in that he does not utter a word in the entire passage. Yet this does not entitle Cain to his action especially that, within the limits of the biblical story, Abel represents half of humanity! Is there any doubt that he is to be the "keeper of his brother"? (v.9)

Whereas Adam was not cursed, Cain is. In the first case, it is the ground that was cursed and thus became difficult for Adam to handle. Whereas here, Cain is "cursed from (by)[54] the ground" itself since the latter, intended to bear life, has been forced into harboring bloodshed (v.11). That is why it will refuse responding to Cain's cultivation, which in turn will force him to move around as an unstable wanderer (v.12). Yet, Cain recognizes his guilt[55] and God ensures the continuity of his human creation by protecting him from any haphazard homicide by anyone who finds him (vv.14-15).

---

[53] It is the same word that is found repeatedly in Ecclesiastes and where it is translated as vanity (passing breath).

[54] The Hebrew preposition *min* bears both connotations.

[55] The Hebrew *'awon* is interesting because it bears both the connotation of wrongdoing and that of its consequence, punishment. So it is more accurate to translate it as guilt (burden) rather than punishment.

Cain lives in the earth into which Adam was expelled, at the east of Eden: "He drove out the man; and *at the east of the garden of Eden* he made dwell the cherubim, and a flaming sword which turned every way, to guard the way to the tree of life... Then Cain went away from the presence of the Lord, and *dwelt* in the earth of Nod, *east of Eden.*" (3:24; 4:16) Besides being a life of hardship, compared with one of enjoyment in the garden,[56] this new life differs in two more aspects: (1) it is a life of wandering and (2) it is away from the tree of life.

The wandering feature lies in the name *Nod* ([earth of] wandering) which is from the same root as *nad* (wanderer):

When you work the ground, it shall no longer yield to you its strength; you shall be a fugitive and a wanderer (*nad*) on the earth." Cain said to the Lord, "My punishment is greater than I can bear. Behold, thou hast driven me this day away from the ground; and from thy face I shall be hidden; and I shall be a fugitive and a wanderer (*nad*) on the earth, and whoever finds me will slay me. Then the Lord said to him, "Not so! If any one slays Cain, vengeance shall be taken on him sevenfold." And the Lord put a mark on Cain, lest any who came upon him should kill him. Then Cain went away from the presence of the Lord, and dwelt in the earth of *Nod*, east of Eden. (4:12-16)

Notice that Cain's earth of "dwelling" (from the root *šakan*) is the earth of his "wandering" situated "at the east of Eden." This means that he is bound to wander outside the garden at whose entrance God "made dwell (from the same root *šakan*) the cherubim, and a flaming sword which turned every way, to

---

[56] Compare 4:11-12 (And now you [Cain] are cursed from the ground...When you work the ground, it shall no longer yield to you its strength) with 3:17-19 (cursed is the ground because of you [Adam]; in toil you shall eat of it all the days of your life; thorns and thistles it shall bring forth to you; and you shall eat the plants of the field. In the sweat of your face you shall eat bread till you return to the ground).

guard the way to the tree of life" (3:24) which "the Lord God made to grow in the midst of the garden" (2:9). This is an eternal reminder that the human beings should have been dwelling where the cherubim were made to dwell instead.

The Progeny of Cain

Genesis 4:17-24 has a double function. On the one hand, it shows that indeed God's blessing is still working in spite of man's misbehavior: "Cain knew his wife, and she conceived and bore Enoch" (v.17) just as "Adam knew Eve his wife, and she conceived and bore Cain" (v.1). On the other hand, however, the path chosen by man takes him farther away from the original setting of the garden where everything needed was provided by God and the little work man did was for enjoyment. The path of man led him to civilization whose most grandiose expression is the (imperial) city[57] that will ultimately stand arrogantly against God (11:1-9). It is as though factually Cain tried to circumvent God's decision to have him "dwell" in a "land of wandering" and decided to "dwell" in a city of his own making.

Eve's reaction to her having conceived and given birth is to acknowledge that the child is the gift of God rather than her own making: "I have gotten a man with (the help of) the Lord." (4:1). Instead of Eve's attitude of thanksgiving, Cain's reaction to his wife's bearing was thus: "and he built a city, and called the name of the city after the name of his son, Enoch." (v.17). The intended extreme irony can be seen in the name Enoch from the root *ḥnk* which has the connotation of "dedication."[58] Instead of

---

[57] Civilization and city are from the same root in the original Latin.
[58] *ḥanukkah* (Hanukkah), which is the Feast of the (Re)dedication of the Temple under the Maccabees, comes from the same root.

getting the clue from his son's name and dedicating him back to God, Cain makes his son, who is as much God's gift *as he himself is*, into a city. Cain, the man of (living) flesh, begets a man of (dead) stone! Instead of flesh formed out of clay from the ground through the blessing of procreation, Cain's legacy becomes, by choice, one of stone, a propensity that ultimately will be corrected by God at the end of the scriptural odyssey in a terminology reminiscent of the first chapters of Genesis:

> And I will give them one heart, and put a new spirit within them; I will take the stony heart out of their flesh and give them a heart of flesh, that they may walk in my statutes and keep my ordinances and obey them; and they shall be my people, and I will be their God. But as for those whose heart goes after their detestable things and their abominations, I will requite their deeds upon their own heads, says the Lord God. (Ezek 11:19-21)

> Therefore I will judge you, O house of Israel, every one according to his ways, says the Lord God. Repent and turn from all your transgressions, lest iniquity be your ruin. Cast away from you all the transgressions which you have committed against me, and get yourselves a new heart and a new spirit! Why will you die, O house of Israel? For I have no pleasure in the death of any one, says the Lord God; so turn, and live. (Ezek 18:31-32)

> I will sprinkle clean water upon you, and you shall be clean from all your uncleannesses, and from all your idols I will cleanse you. A new heart I will give you, and a new spirit I will put within you; and I will take out of your flesh the heart of stone and give you a heart of flesh. And I will put my spirit within you, and cause you to walk in my statutes and be careful to observe my ordinances. (Ezek 36:25-27)

This sad state of affairs is carried through until the seventh generation of Cain's progeny, that is, until its fullest extent with

God's approval and under his control.[59] As in Genesis 2 with the building of woman and in 1 Samuel 8 with the rise of kingship, God allows Cain's decision to take its course in order to show the hearers the calamitous end of such. The series of names is reflective of the fact that Cain's progeny is furthering his way: follow man's own will disregarding God's initial plan. The name of Enoch's son, Irad (*'irad*), is a combination of the noun *'ir* (city) and the verb *radah* (rule [over], have dominion [over]); thus the son of Enoch was to rule over the city named after his father.[60] The following in line is Mehujael (*meḥuya'el*) meaning "what he undertakes will be erased (they will erase)," and his son's name Methushael (*metuša'el*) means "what he asks for will die," reflecting the biblical end of the city (Samaria and Jerusalem). As for Lemech (*lemek*)[61] it is a play on the Hebrew noun *melek* (king) through metathesis.[62] My reading is corroborated by two extra features related to him. On the one hand, he had more than one wife, which was a kingly prerogative, as one can see from the example of Saul (2 Sam 12:7-8), David (2 Sam 5:13; 12:11; 19:5), Solomon (1 Kg 10:8; 11:1-4), Rehoboam (2 Chr 11:21), Ahab (1 Kg 20:3-7), and

---

[59] For the value of the numerical 7, see the Excursus on Number Symbolism in *NTI₃* 22-28. As for God's allowing events to happen against His express will, see Gen 2 and 1 Sam 8.

[60] *'irad* from *'ir-rad* without the repetition of the letter *r*. Keeping the final *h* of *radah* would have resulted in a feminine proper noun.

[61] Unfortunately the traditional English Lamech, starting with the King James Version, is incorrect. Lamech (*lamek*) is found only in Gen 4:18. In the following four instances of the same name (vv.19, 23 [twice], 25) we have the Hebrew *lemek* (Lemech). This is repeated in Gen 5:25-31 where the first instance in v.25 is *lamek* whereas the following four (vv.26, 28, 30, 31) are invariably *lemek*. The first instance in each passage is due to the fact that the personal noun is the last word of the verse. In this case, in Hebrew, we have what is called the pausal form where the vowel of the accented syllable in the word is lengthened, in this case from the short *e* to a long *ā*.

[62] Metathesis is the switch in place between two consonants in the same word.

Jehoiachin (2 Kg 24:15). On the other hand, in his statement to his wives he acts as a judge, the way a king—and thus a god[63]— would: he emits a verdict of death: "I have slain a man for wounding me, a young man for striking me. If Cain is avenged sevenfold, truly Lemech seventy-sevenfold." (Gen 4:23-24) Notice how Lemech takes de facto the place of God. In the case of Cain, it is God who is the avenger (v.15). In doing so, Lemech commits the ultimate blasphemy of which the kings of Judah and Israel were culprits (Ezek 34). The two most striking examples are David taking the life of Uriah (2 Sam 11:14-15) and Ahab taking that of Naboth (1 Kg 21:1-16).

Cain's wish to build a city to protect himself ends with the rise of kingship that will destroy it. This is nothing else than the biblical story in nutshell.

Yet, there is another path for humanity, if it so chooses, which is suggested in the parallel genealogy via Seth, who is clearly presented as both an alternative to Cain and his nemesis since he takes the place of Abel, whom Cain slew. Notice the parallelism in terminology, reflecting as it were a new start:

Now Adam (*ha'adam*; the man)[64] knew Eve his wife, and she conceived and bore Cain, saying, "I have gotten a man with the help of the Lord." (Gen 4:1)

And Adam (*'adam*)[65] knew his wife again, and she bore a son and called his name Seth (*šet*), for she said, "God has appointed (*šat*)[66] for me another child instead of Abel, for Cain slew him." (Gen 4:25)

---

[63] Notice the use of "seven" and "seventy seven," reflective of the divine.

[64] I shall deal momentarily with the difference between *ha'adam* in v.1 and *'adam* in v.25.

[65] See previous note.

[66] Both *šet* and *šat* are from the same Hebrew root meaning "place, set, appoint."

In contradistinction to both Cain and Seth, Abel is introduced summarily without the mention of Adam knowing Eve: "And again, she bore his brother Abel." (v.2) However, Seth is presented as taking the place of Abel (*hebel*), an indication to the hearer that the will of God was "set"[67] in the way he originally had it: the human being is a mere *hebel* (vanishing breath) and should never endeavor to become a king "like God." This is the teaching of Genesis 2-3. My understanding is corroborated in that Seth produces Enosh (*'enoš*), which is the other Hebrew word for human being.[68] The complete cycle[69] is thus "man sets (another) man, and so on and so forth." It is this true man Enosh, the son of Seth, son of Adam, who is *the* man said to have initiated the true worship of the Lord: "At that time began the calling upon the name of the Lord." In other words, these genealogies offer the two paths with two very different ways of life: (1) relying on God's earth, of which humanity is an integral part, and thus on God Himself, or (2) in contradistinction, relying on oneself and one's accomplishments of stone. Here again, in the two alternative genealogies of Genesis 4, looms the specter of Ezekiel, the son of man, and his teaching against the city and its king, the son of God. And, Genesis, following Ezekiel's lead, will opt for the former possibility, that of Seth over that of Cain, as will become clear in the following genealogy where Adam begets Seth (Gen 5:3).

---

[67] See previous note.

[68] From the same root as the Hebrew *'iš* (man, male human being) whose plural *'anašim* has the additional letter *n* found in *'enoš*. Similarly, *'iššah*, the singular feminine of *'iš*, has the plural form *našim*.

[69] Three is the numeral expressing fullness and "indeed-ness." It is the lowest plural numeral beyond the numeral two (the dual in Semitic languages) reflecting an either-or situation. Semitic languages, just as ancient Greek, have the singular, the dual, and the plural in their verbal conjugations.

The toledot *of Adam*

Looking ahead at the series of *toledot*, one will readily notice that each subsequent *toledot* is that of an element in the progeny of the previous *toledot*. Thus, the *toledot* of Adam is followed by the *toledot* of Noah, a descendant of Adam, which is followed by the *toledot* of Shem, Ham, and Japheth, the sons of Noah. The *toledot* of Terah, a descendant of Shem, follows the *toledot* of the latter. It is in that perspective that one is to deal with the *toledot* of Adam in Genesis 5. The human being is an element of the heavens and the earth whose *toledot* was presented in the previous chapters 1-4. Put otherwise, the human being was not *a*, let alone *the*, topic in those chapters, and this is precisely the mistake of classical theology, which was influenced by Platonic philosophy, where by and large scriptural texts were read anthropologically, as though the human being was the center of the universe and God's concern. It is precisely against such human arrogance consistently critiqued by the prophets that the biblical author relegated talking about Adam as a subject matter until Genesis 5.

This intentionality is transparent in that, when repeating Genesis 1:27-28 in 5:1-2, the author moves from the generic *ha'adam* (the man) to the particular (individual) *'adam* (Adam), thus indicating that here in ch.5 he is dealing with an individual human being, which fits perfectly the understanding of *toledot*. To be sure, the Hebrew *'adam* always bears the connotation of human being in general. One can see that in its use in Genesis 1:26 and 2:5, that is, in the first time reference is made to the human being in each of the creation narratives; still, within the narratives themselves we always hear of *ha'adam*. However, in ch.5, the use of *'adam* is systematic. Furthermore, that this individualization process was on the mind of the author throughout 5:1-5 is evident in that he uses *'adam* as the name of both the male and the female, just before he proceeds to tell us that *'adam* begat Seth: "Male and female he created them, and he blessed them and named them Man (*'adam*) when they were created. When Adam (*'adam*) had lived a hundred and thirty years, he became the father of a son in his own likeness, after his image, and named him Seth." (vv.2-3)[70] The shift from *ha'adam* as father of Cain in 4:1 to *'adam* as father of Seth in 5:1 appears smooth because the author has deftly prepared for it in that it is *'adam*, and not *ha'adam*, who inseminates Eve in 4:25, the parallel to 4:1.[71] In so doing, the author has already betrayed his preference for Seth, and not Cain, as the first in the chain of the *toledot* of Adam. Thus, Genesis 4:25 looks forward to 5:1 as well as harks back to 4:1, and thus functions as the bridge between *ha'adam* as an element in the *toledot* of the heavens and the earth and *'adam* as the subject matter of his own *toledot*.

Probably the most important indication that attests to the fact that Adam is only an element in the story of Genesis 1-4 and not the subject matter is the occurrence of the term "book," which is virtually never discussed or, at least, given importance. So much classical theology is hung up on anthropology that it ends up using the Bible, not hearing it. The usual phrase to introduce a given *toledot* is "(and) these are the *toledot* of..."[72] even when applied to that of the heavens and the earth (Gen 2:4). The sole exception is Genesis 5:1: "This is the book of the generations of Adam." What makes the matter even more striking is that the term *šepher* (book) occurs only here in Genesis while its

---

[70] Notice how RSV was forced to shift from Man in v.2 to Adam in v.3, whereas in the original it is the same *'adam*.

[71] See earlier.

[72] See Gen 6:9; 10:1; 11:10, 27; 25:12, 19; 36:1, 9; 46:8.

following instance is not found until Exodus 17:14! This can hardly be coincidental, let alone irrelevant. The author seems to be adamant to draw the hearer's attention to the fact that, starting with Genesis 5:1, we are not only "turning the page," but actually moving to "another book"—and thus "another story"—in comparison with chs.1-4. Put otherwise, to speak of Adam as a starting point, or the subject matter, one is to begin with Genesis 5:1. The previous chapters are "another story;" they deal not with Adam but with the heavens and the earth.[73]

Adam's "story" (*toledot*) is presented magisterially as one of tension between God's plan for man and the latter's will for himself. Man is consistently in a "self-destruct mode," whereas God tries to show him a way out of it. Let us analyze in some detail this section (Gen 5:1-6:8). First, it is presented as an expanded version (ten generations) of the short genealogy of Adam through Seth (three generations). Whereas the numeral three expresses factual fullness under divine aegis, the numeral ten (and its multiples 100; 1000; 10,000) represents the total human enterprise.[74] The good start initiated by God (5:1-2) ends in disaster due to human hubris (6:1-7). Again the ultimate expression of that hubris is kingship which consistently yearns to move from functional to actual divinity, as we have seen in both the stories of Adam (Gen 1-3) and Cain (Gen 4). In so doing, it ends up putting at risk of hardship, even elimination, God's entire creation (6:7; compare with Gen 3:14-19).

The passage on Adam sets the tone for the rest of the story in that it has two features proper to it. The first feature is that it recalls the terminology used in Genesis 1:26-28 to describe the

---

[73] This conclusion, in turn, should relegate under a question mark anthropological treatises that begin with, let alone deal exclusively with, Genesis 1-3.

[74] See the Excursus on Number Symbolism in *NTI₃* 22-28.

beginning of humanity *within* the context of the earth and all that it contains (1:2-30): "When God created man, he made him in the likeness of God. Male and female he created them, and he blessed them and named them Man when they were created." (5:1b-2). The second feature is that what God did through the act of creation, Adam does through the act of begetting: "When Adam had lived a hundred and thirty years, he begat (became the father of) a son in his own likeness, after his image, and named him Seth." (v.3). The author is iterating what he said in ch.1 namely, the blessing lies in the potential of begetting. In contemporary terms, in his creating the human being God has set up the DNA mechanism so that he need not intervene at every birth. However, man himself remains a being "from dust to dust" needing to secure his progeny within his life span; once he has secured such through his first-born son, the existence, let alone number, of the other children is irrelevant. That is why Adam's life is divided into before and after the birth of Seth:

> When Adam had lived a hundred and thirty years, he begat a son in his own likeness, after his image, and named him Seth. The days of Adam after he begat Seth were eight hundred years; and he had other sons and daughters. Thus all the days that Adam lived were nine hundred and thirty years; and he died. (5:3-5)

The same pattern recurs in the description of the life of his descendants with the omission of "in his own likeness, after his image," which was necessary only in the case of Seth. The monotonous yet rhythmic repetition word for word of the same phraseology throughout ch.5 is intended to produce in the hearer's ear and mind the impression of what I termed "the DNA mechanism."

What about the extraordinary life spans? They should be read against the background of the Ancient Near Eastern Sumerian, Akkadian, and Babylonian King Lists. Those lists include the names of kings that ruled famous cities for extravagant, even astronomical, periods of time. The intention was to push backward into times immemorial the dynasty or dynasties that ruled a given city in order to uphold its perpetuity, which in turn spoke of the greatness and power of that city's deity. The biblical author's anti-kingly stand made him mimic this approach, albeit on the level of a mere human being. Thus, as in Genesis 1:26-28, the biblical God is in no need of mighty kings, "sons of God," to rule his world; he can do that as well through mere "sons of man." Yet, just as Adam and his progeny faltered in Genesis 2-3 and 4, so does it falter even more miserably here. In spite of the fact that God carried the human race through ten generations amounting to 8125 years, he is forced to regret having created what he did and decided to obliterate it (6:1-7)! However, Adam's *toledot* offers more than meets the eye at first glance. A closer look will reveal that the newly introduced Noah as well as Enoch and Lemech, the two names taken over from Cain's "family tree," play a special role in giving a few twists to that otherwise iterative genealogy. These twists are interrelated as well as essential from the purview of the biblical story.

I showed earlier that, in Cain's genealogy, Enoch (*ḥanok*) has been hijacked by his father Cain to function against his original destiny: instead of acknowledging him as a gift from God and dedicating him to this same God, Cain opted to dedicate him to the name of the city Cain built. In Adam's genealogy, Enoch recovers his true destiny. Although he lasts much less than the others in his family tree, he nevertheless lives the fullness of life expressed in the number 365, a "full" year (Gen 5:23). This is due to the fact that he lived up to his name by "dedicating" his

life to God, a point brought up twice in the passage dealing with
him: "Enoch walked with God after the birth of Methuselah
three hundred years… Enoch walked with God." (5:22, 24)
Furthermore, instead of the phrase "and he died," used with the
other patriarchs before as well as after him, we are told that "and
he was not, for God took him" (v.24). Thus, Enoch is presented
as "the man" who lived according to God's will and,
consequently, "did not die," but he went to abide with God,
thus realizing the destiny assigned originally to "the man" (Gen
2-3). Enoch's uniqueness is further reflected in that he occupies
in the genealogy position number seven, which is the full divine
number in contradistinction with the numeral ten, which is the
full human number. In other words, the fullness of any human
story is at hand when and whenever God's will is implemented.
However, man is allowed to proceed on his own way, if he so
chooses. Later, Israel will reach the land, promised by God the
King of Israel, and should have been satisfied; but it will decide
to proceed its own way by requesting a human king (1 Sam 8).
Just as later the post-Samuel period or "route" will end with
annihilation through exile, from a nationhood perspective, the
post-Enoch period or "route" will end with Noah, in whose time
God threatens the man and the earth with annihilation (Gen
6:1-8).

   This "route" is already initiated with Methuselah (*metušelaḥ*;
Gen 5:22, 25-27) whose name means "(someone) sends his
death" or "(someone) sends (him) to his death." This will
happen via Lemech who keeps the penultimate position in
Adam's genealogy, which was his in Cain's. He also keeps the
same function, that of the "king (son of God)" who acts
willfully, and not according to God's will. Compared to Enoch's
full human lifespan of 365 years, Lemech's covers 777 years, the

triple seven being the reflection of the divine.[75] However, just as Enoch in Cain's genealogy ended up by not being as he was supposed to be, here in Adam's genealogy it is Lemech who takes the role of not being what he appears to be. His life(span) looks perfect, but it is just phony perfection, the real one having been attained by Enoch who lived as a "son of man." The play on "son of man" versus "son of God" will be picked up in Genesis 6:1-8 and, as we shall see, will remain throughout the Bible as the choice that Noah and his descendants will have to deal with time and again. Another dig at the kingly institution and its "length of years" can be detected in Lemech's age of 182 when he begets Noah. This number is the half of 365. The author may well have been intending to say that Lemech's real value was in his progeny Noah,[76] and that he actually accomplished his mission in life when he was just half the age of Enoch who was perfected, as it were, at age 365. Yet Lemech proceeded to reach the age of 777, the seemingly divine perfection, the test and eventual pitfall for all kings.

However, the author already plants in the hearer's mind the seed of the thought that the last word will be God's and not man's. He does so by ending Adam's genealogy, beyond Methuselah and Lemech, with Noah in the tenth position. Ten being the numeral of the full human story, we shall momentarily witness the virtual annihilation of all life on earth. Still, Noah stands out, already at birth, as the sign of assuredness that God will ultimately intervene to salvage life on earth. Noah is, in Adam's genealogy, the only descendant whose naming is introduced the way Cain's and Seth's were in the previous genealogies (4:1, 25). However, the difference lies in that,

---

[75] See previous note.
[76] See below on Noah.

whereas the naming of Cain and Seth is linked to their birth, the text concerning the naming of Noah not only "looks ahead" but does so beyond the catastrophe:

> When Lemech had lived a hundred and eighty-two years, he became the father of a son, and called his name Noah, saying, "Out of the ground (*min ha'damah*)[77] which the Lord has *cursed* [78] this one shall bring us relief (*yenaḥamenu*) from our work and from the toil (*'iṣṣabon*)[79] of our hands." (5:28-29)

Since the terminology is clearly reminiscent of Genesis 2-3, the hope is the reversal of the curse that befell Adam. However, the play on words is very astute and helps to build the bridge between the curse of the earth in Adam's time, the impending annihilation of the earth, and the promise of a fresh start beyond both disasters. Instead of playing on the root of the Hebrew personal name, as was the case with Cain and Seth, the author changes the name root by adding a letter to *noaḥ* (Noah) introducing thus a new root *nḥm* (consolation; relief) instead of the expected *nḥ* (rest; enjoyment).[80] On the one hand, the root of the name itself harks back to when God put Adam "to enjoy himself" in the garden (Gen 2:15); yet it also looks ahead beyond the flood to when Noah will have enough respite on earth to plant a vineyard (9:20). On the other hand, the introduced root *nḥm* prepares the hearer not to lose hope when God will announce his will to annihilate the earth, since the verb used to

---

[77] Gen 2:7, 9, 19

[78] See Gen 3:17.

[79] See Gen 3:17.

[80] My readers are reminded that in Hebrew the alphabet is made only of consonants (our vowels are just vocalic sounds in Hebrew and do not count especially when it comes to the root of a word). Consequently, adding or subtracting a letter is of momentous value.

describe God's repentance (feeling sorry) of having made man (6:6) is also *nḥm*.[81]

Noah in Adam's Genealogy

It is not Noah himself, the tenth member of Adam's genealogy, who heralds the success of God's "blessing," but rather the fact that Noah begat three children through whom that blessing will be carried on to the entire humanity in all its peoples (Gen 11). Once more, biblically, however saintly the individual is, he remains "dust to dust," a "passing breath (*nepheš*; soul)." God's blessing is functional inasmuch as there are still around a few "living breaths (souls)" that are "praising the Lord" (Ps 150:6). It is precisely against this background that is to be read and understood the seemingly "hanging" passage (Gen 6:1-8) linking Noah's *toledot* (6:9-9:28) to that of Adam, and yet still, literarily speaking, part of the latter (5:1-6:8).

Yet, before engaging Genesis 6:1-8, it would behoove us to clear our way through the intricate and complex structure of the section concerning the adult Noah (5:32-9:29). This section straddles three different units: Adam's genealogy, Noah's *toledot*, and the flood story. The opening statement (And Noah turned five hundred years old, and Noah begat Shem, Ham, and Japheth; 5:32) and the closing sentence (After the flood Noah lived three hundred and fifty years, and he died; 9:28-29) fit, with minor variations, the pattern used in Adam's genealogy. The two differences, though, are: (1) all three of Noah's children are lumped together, and (2) the reference to the start of the second part of Noah's life is not the birth of his eldest, but rather (the end of) the flood. The conclusion is that the author intentionally included the flood as merely a passing event which,

---

[81] More on this below when I shall discuss Gen 6:1-8.

in spite of its magnitude, was not able to overcome God's blessing that succeeded in making the individual Adam (5:1-5) produce all the nations of the earth (Gen 10). This belittling of the importance of the flood is further evident in that it is actually fully contained (6:11-8:32) within the *toledot* of the individual Noah (6:9-9:29).

Genesis 6:1-8, describing the unruliness taking place during the lifetime of Lemech's progeny, is an interesting passage that allows the author to criticize openly the monarchy's uncontrolled power. Lemech's descendants behave the way kings, the "sons of God," do, choosing as their consorts whomever they will from among their subjects, the "daughters of men," with impunity. Might is right or so they thought until the only true King, the Lord, decides to intervene and judge (Ps 82). His spirit with which he anoints his kings (Saul in 1 Sam 10:6, 10; 11:6; David in 16:13) can, whenever necessary, also come in judgment over the same king (Saul in 1 Sam 16:14-15, 23).[82] The shortening of years from the nine hundreds to one hundred twenty (Gen 6:3) is clearly an anti-kingly statement. The king who lives "forever" through his dynasty (Ps 45:16-17; see also Ps 72:15-17) is brought down to the level of any "flesh" (Gen 6:3) ending at death. (This is precisely what will happen to Saul upon his death without a dynasty to carry on his "name."[83]) My reading is corroborated in the following verse: "The Nephilim were on the earth in those days, *and also afterward*, when the sons of God came in to the daughters of men, and they bore children to them. These were the mighty men (*haggibborim*) that were

---

[82] RSV has the unwarranted "spirit *from* God."
[83] Psalm 45:16-17 (Instead of your fathers shall be your sons; you will make them princes in all the earth. I will cause your name to be celebrated in all generations; therefore the peoples will praise you forever and ever).

(from) of old (me'olam), the men of renown (šem; name)." (Gen
6:4) The terminology is both one of unstoppable might and
kingly protocol. The Nephilim are those who fell (naphal) others
given their overwhelming size (Num 13:33). The "mighty ones"
are the kingly fighting elite (1 Sam 14:52; 2 Sam 23:22-29; Am
2:16). As for the couple "(from) of old" and "also afterward,"
they fit perfectly the dynastic vocabulary.

God's reaction toward man's unabashed "kingly" takeover of
the earth is extreme ire, as in the prophetic literature. However
the phraseology of Genesis 6:6 describing the Lord's feelings is
very interesting in that it prepares for the good news of probable
hope heralded in v.8 (But Noah found favor in the eyes of the
Lord) which are the last words of Adam's *toledot*. Just before the
Lord's contemplating to blot out the earth and all living beings
on it (v.7), we hear: "And the Lord was sorry (yinnahem) that he
had made man on the earth, and it grieved (yit'aseb) him to his
heart." (v.6) What is translated as "was sorry" is from the same
verbal root as yenahamenu (shall bring us relief) in 5:29, whereas
what is translated as "grieved" is from the same root as 'issabon
(toil) found in the same verse 5:29. The exquisitely crafted text
gives the impression to its hearer in Hebrew that God himself
decided to take upon himself the "toil" which is supposed to be
the lot of the human beings (Gen 3:17).[84] He would do this by
planning to implement through Noah relief to the human beings
by being sorry for his own action, that is, by taking control of his
creation away from man and starting it all over under his own
control. This will be expressed later in the unilateral covenant of
the rainbow. His decision is underscored in that his "being
sorry" is repeated as the reason for what he is about to undertake

[84] The same 'issabon is found in Gen 5:29 and 3:17. Its third instance in the entire
Bible occurs in Gen 3:16 in reference to the "pain" of childbearing.

through the medium of Noah: "I will blot out man whom I have created from the face of the ground, man and beast and creeping things and birds of the air, for I am sorry (*niḥamti*) that I have made them." (6:7) Why should God blot *all* creation when one human being, Noah, is found to be to his liking (v.8)?[85] We have here the root of what Paul later will refer to as salvation by sheer grace (Hebrew *ḥen*; Greek *kharis*): so it pleased God. This explains Paul's thanksgiving phrase when it comes to the unfathomable graceful action of God: *kharis tō theō*, literally "grace be to God," "the grace is (to be recognized as) God's." [86]

Consequently, Enoch is the corrective counterpart to Adam. His way of life, if followed by human beings, will prove to be the guarantee for the continuation of all life on God's earth. This will soon be confirmed in that Noah, who will survive the flood that threatened all life on earth, is introduced as one who "walked (*hithallek*) with God" (6:9) just as Enoch did. Where Adam failed, Noah succeeded by following in the footsteps of Enoch. Enoch is so perfect that in him is realized the original promise given to Adam: should he abide by God's command, he would not die. Indeed in Genesis 5 all the patriarchs, including Noah (9:29), die at the end of their earthly life. Of Enoch it is simply written: "and he was not, *for* God took (received) him." (5:24) That is to say, because he "walked with God" during his life on God's earth, God did not strike him with the penalty with which he struck Adam and his progeny.

---

[85] This is the meaning of "finding favor" (*maṣa' ḥen*) in Hebrew.
[86] Rom 6:17; 7:25; 2 Cor 9:15. The last instance corroborates my reading since we are told the reason, God's *dōrea* (gift), the noun parallel to *kharis* in the Pauline writings: "Thanks (*kharis*; grace) be to God for his inexpressible gift (*dōrea*)!"

2

Noah and the Flood

Noah

More often than not we are used to referring to Genesis 6:5-9:17, or at least 6:5-8:22, as being the flood story. This stand goes hand in hand with that which views Genesis 1-3 as the creation story. However, both these approaches are forced upon the biblical text from a systematic perspective that starts with an assumed topic, such as creation, flood, and the like, and, in so doing, impose a structure alien to the original intent. Such approaches disrupt the inner texture of the original literature and end up, willy-nilly, reading into the text rather than hearing it out. This process of "historicizing" scripture, that is to say, reading it as though it covers subsequent periods of human history, is evident in the Septuagint "canon" when compared to the Hebrew "canon." What was originally meant as a textual "before" and "after" became a chronology. The Torah, known also as "Moses," one book in five unnamed volumes,[1] became the Pentateuch divided into five books with specific names: Genesis, Exodus, Leviticus, Numbers, and Deuteronomy. This tendency is at its clearest in the second part of the Hebrew canon, the *nebi'im* (Prophets), which is divided into two sections, the *nebi'im rišonim* (Prior Prophets)[2] and the *nebi'im 'aharonim* (Latter Prophets).[3] From "prophetic" books, Joshua, Judges,

---

[1] The Jewish tradition refers to each simply by the first word(s) of the volume.
[2] Joshua, Judges, (1 and 2) Samuel and (1 and 2) Kings.
[3] Isaiah, Jeremiah, Ezekiel, and the Scroll of the Twelve (Minor) Prophets.

Samuel, and Kings, were transformed into "historical" books, as
one can see from the following three features of the Septuagint
canon: (1) Ruth, which in the Hebrew is a book pertaining to
the third part of the Bible, the *ketubim* (Writings or [Other]
Scriptures), appears between Judges and Samuel, since it deals
with the "ancestry" of David whose story is found in 1 Samuel;
(2) for the same reason of "historicizing," the Books of
Chronicles, which appear last in the Hebrew canon at the end of
the *ketubim*, are transposed right after Kings, since they deal with
the same "period" covered by Genesis through Kings; (3) on the
other hand, Samuel and Kings become the four books of the
"Kingdoms," thus perceived as dealing with chronological
periods rather than individual stories. The practical consequence
was that, whenever one hears the term "exodus" one rushes to
the Book of Exodus assuming that it is there that one finds the
primary information regarding that "historical event." In doing
so, one is unconsciously relegating the exodus material in
scripture (Isaiah, Jeremiah, Ezekiel, Hosea, Psalms) as secondary,
thus creating an unwarranted textual hierarchy within scripture.[4]

It is no wonder then that Genesis 6-9 or 6-8 have come to be
entitled "the flood" when, textually speaking, they are the *toledot*
of Noah following the *toledot* of Adam and preceding the *toledot*
of Shem, Ham, and Japheth. The topic of those chapters is not
the flood, but the biblical "story of Noah" (Gen 6:9-9:28) *within
whose confines* we hear about the shaming of Noah (9:18-27) as
well as about the flood (6:9-8:22) and subsequent covenant
(6:18; 9:1-17). Even the artificial separation between the flood
and the covenant is unwarranted in the text that links them

---

[4] The same phenomenon can be seen in how often we handle the Gospels in
comparison with the rest of the New Testament. An extreme case is the translations
that create an artificial hierarchy within the one Gospel Book between the "words of
Jesus" printed in red and the other "Gospel words."

intimately right from the beginning: "For behold, I will bring a flood of waters upon the earth, to destroy all flesh in which is the breath of life from under heaven; everything that is on the earth shall die. But I will establish my covenant with you; and you shall come into the ark, you, your sons, your wife, and your sons' wives with you." (6:17-18) This kind of linkage between the so-called "bad news" and the so-called "good news" is not unique since we witnessed it a few verses earlier in Genesis 6:5-8 where the announcement of the divine decision of total annihilation culminates with the logically *unexpected* "But Noah found favor in the eyes of the Lord." This scriptural, and not necessarily logical, feature is not haphazard, but actually a pattern as is evident in the literature of the Latter Prophets.

Consequently, in order to remain faithful to the intention of the text, it behooves us to speak of Noah rather than of the flood. Even then, one should be careful not to start with the assumed Noah as an extra-textual individual and then consider the textual information as just a few elements in his life. To the contrary, whatever the text tells us and *how* it does so is the "total" Noah. When hearing the textual data one cannot escape the fact that the most striking feature of the biblical Noah is that, in all the stories related to him, he appears together with his three sons: (1) within Adam's *toledot* (Gen 5:32); (2) right at the beginning of his *toledot* (6:10); (3) throughout the section on the flood (6:21; 7:7; 8:16, 18); (4) in conjunction with the covenant (6:18; 9:1, 7-16); and (5) in the story of Noah's shaming (9:18-27). The repetition in 6:10 of the same "Noah begat Shem, Ham, and Japheth" found earlier in 5:32 and sealing it with the addition "three sons," after which we do not hear about other sons and daughters as in the case of the other patriarchs, is evidence that the feature is intentional on the author's part.

The author's intention can be gathered from the total context, especially the way he handles Noah's lifespan in comparison with that of the other patriarchs. Instead of one time marker, the birth of the firstborn before the total number of years (5:1-28), here we have two markers, the "birth" of the three sons (500 years; 5:29) and the "beginning" of the flood (600 years; 7:6). However, these two markers are brought together in the total statement linked with the start of the flood: "Noah was six hundred years old when the flood of waters came upon the earth. And Noah *and his sons* and his wife *and his sons' wives with him* went into the ark, to escape the waters of the flood." (7:6-7) Now one can see the importance of the intentional repetition of the mention of Noah's begetting (5:32; 6:10). It is the 100 year old *total* progeny of Noah that survived the exterminating flood, which was thus bound to the decision of God to allow the human beings to live up to "a hundred and twenty years" (6:3). My reading is corroborated in that, later, Shem the eldest is said to have been only "a hundred years old" when he "begat Arpachshad two years after the flood" (11:10). Although we are told that "Shem lived after the birth of Arpachshad five hundred years, and had other sons and daughters," still the future of humanity was already secured. Again the intentionality of this new pattern is evident in that the following descendants begat while they were in their thirties (11:12-23)—Nahor even at twenty-nine (v.24)—with the exception of Terah who was seventy, still well before a hundred and twenty. Between Enosh "the man" and Enoch who "walked with God," some patriarchs begat at the "young" age of less than a hundred (5:9-21). God's promised and enacted covenant is firmly established. Thus, as I indicated earlier, the flood narrative is a passing event framed within God's resolve to "take full responsibility" for having created the human beings. It is, as the prophetic books will make clear, God's classic fatherly punishment unto instruction in order to give the human beings an extra chance to avoid his eventual final punishment unto destruction. The extra chance is for each of them to behave according to God's will even in the shorter time frame of one hundred twenty years.

The hearers of scripture already know that the flood did not end by exterminating humanity, since they themselves are well and alive. So the main point of the story is to inform us as to why the positive resolution of the tension comes through Noah. The scriptural author deftly introduces him as the main character by splitting the one statement, which sets him apart from the rest of the sinful humankind, into two parts that straddle the end of Adam's *toledot* and the beginning of Noah's: "But Noah found favor in the eyes of the Lord. These are the *toledot* of Noah. Noah was a righteous man, blameless in his generation; Noah walked with God. And Noah had three sons, Shem, Ham, and Japheth." (Gen 6:8-10) Noah's having found favor in the Lord's eyes closes Adam's *toledot*, but the reason behind this favor is given at the start of Noah's *toledot*.[5] The author further explicates the meaning of the phrase "walk with God" he already used twice in conjunction with Enoch. "Walking with God" ensures that one be accounted righteous (*ṣaddiq*) and blameless (*tamim*). The first is a legal term and is used throughout scripture to qualify someone who lives according to God's law and thus is declared innocent of any wrongdoing in the court of the righteous judge. The second is a cultic term used to speak of the sacrifices and the priests who offer them: both are to be in a state

---

[5] The centrality of Noah is also reflected textually to the hearing: his name is mentioned no less than five times in the span of three verses. It sounds as though the author intentioned to drill that name, which means enjoyable rest, into the hearer's ears.

of "sane completeness" without any missing or blemished limb in the presence of God.[6] Thus, Noah is presented as perfect on two levels, the legal and the cultic, meaning that God had nothing whatsoever against him. And, if so, then God would have looked unrighteous had he condemned Noah and his progeny together with the rest of humanity. Such is utterly impossible, "for then how could God judge the world" (Rom 3:6) as he does in Psalm 82?

Noah proved to be both righteous and blameless in being obedient to God's command, unlike his predecessor Adam. Noah's obedience is repeatedly pointed out in the flood story through an interesting literary device. His actions following God's directives to build the ark and to enter into it together with all the other beings living on earth (6:13-21) are not described; we are simply told that "Noah did this; he did all that God commanded him" (v.22). The author underscores his intention by repeating the story: at the end of a similar directive by the Lord regarding the pure animals (7:1-4), we hear that "Noah did all that the Lord had commanded him" (v.5). It sounds as though Noah did not "do" anything save be obedient to God; his activity is subsumed in God's words of command to the effect that his obedience *was* his action. This intention on the author's part is evident in his insistence on that matter. Even the actual entrance into the ark is described twice as an action on the part of Noah and his company (7:7-9 and 13-16); twice we are told at the end "as God had commanded Noah (him)" (vv.9 and 16). Actually, in the last instance we hear that it is God himself who consummated and sealed the "actions" of Noah and his companions: "and the Lord closed (the entrance door of the ark) after him." (v.16)

---

[6] See e.g. Lev 1:3, 10; 3:1, 6 for the offered animals, and Lev 21:17-21 for the priests.

The Flood

Both the violence (*ḥamas*; 6:11, 13) and its punishment, the end (*qes*; v.13), are standard prophetic terminology,[7] which indicates that, just as was the case with the *toledot* of Adam as well as that of the heavens and the earth, the flood story is woven with the phraseology reminiscent of the sin of arrogance of the kings of Jerusalem and Samaria. As for the means of salvation from the threatening waters, the venue is the same as that of Moses since the term *tebah* translated as "ark" in Genesis 6-9 is found only twice again, in Exodus 2:3 and 5. RSV is misleading in that it translates into "ark" the *tebah* of Noah and the *'aron* of testimony (Ex 25:16-22), whereas it uses "basket" to speak of the *tebah* that carried the child Moses (Ex 2:3, 5). In fact, the "basket" that saved Moses is similar to the "ark" that saved Noah and his progeny. The close correspondence can be detected in two more features:

1. The word *qinnim* (consonantal *qnym*) in Genesis 6:14 is translated into "rooms" (nests), whereas the same consonantal *qnym* can be vocalized as *qanim*, the plural of *qaneh* meaning "reed." The closeness between the two explains why the Jerusalem Bible translates Gen 6:14 into "Make yourself an ark out of resinous wood. *Make it of reeds* and caulk it with pitch inside and out" instead of "Make yourself an ark of gopher wood; *make rooms in the ark*, and cover it inside and out with pitch" (RSV). On the other hand, another term for "reeds" is *suph*, which is

---

[7] See especially Ezek 7. Also e.g. Am 8:2; Hab 2:3.

the word encountered in Ex 2:3 and 5 to indicate the reeds among which the basket (*tebah*) was laid. [8]

2. The care with which each *tebah* is prepared against the eventually inimical waters: "Make yourself an ark of gopher wood; make rooms in the ark (make it of reeds), and *cover it inside and out with pitch*" (Gen 6:14); "And when she could hide him no longer she took for him a basket made of bulrushes, and *daubed it with bitumen and pitch*." (Ex 2:3)[9]

God's intent of a severe fatherly punishment unto instruction rather than a judge's verdict unto obliteration is sealed in that, immediately after the announcement of the devastating flood, we hear of the first scriptural mention of a covenant: "But I will establish my covenant with you." (Gen 6:18) Later, in ch.9, we shall learn that this covenant is binding on God alone, which confirms my reading of Genesis 6:6-7 as reflective of God's taking full responsibility for his having created the earth and all that lives on it. An essential aspect of the divine instruction is that it was not easy for God to redress the calamity in which man's sin has jeopardized the entire earth. The hearer cannot escape both the lengthiness of the flood story line and the tentativeness of its resolution. Forty days of flooding that gradually submerges the entire earth (7:17-23) are followed by 150 days of full submersion (v.24), at the end of which God happens to remember Noah and the animals (8:1). The reversal of the flood takes another 150 days during which the waters abated and the ark came to rest on Mount Ararat (vv.3-4), after

---

[8] It is also the word used to qualify the "sea of reeds" which the Israelites traversed upon their leaving Egypt. Consequently, the connection is not only between Noah and Moses, but also indirectly between Noah and Israel.

[9] This protection against the waters, in turn, looks ahead to Israel's exodus from Egypt.

which two and half months are needed for barely the tops of other mountains to be seen (vv.4-5). Even then, it is only forty days later that Noah dares to "open the window of the ark" (v.6). The released crow kept "going to and fro" an indefinite amount of time "until the waters were dried up from the earth" (v.7). Then came the turn of the dove, sign of God's peace, which peace ensures that the earth become a "*manoah*[10] (resting place) for the sole of the foot," but no such rest was to be found (v.9). It took seven days and then another seven days for the earth to become again habitable (vv.10-12) as God intended it to be originally (1:9-13). It took God one full year (7:6; 8:13) to commit his instructional punishment and turn the page to initiate a fresh start on the first day of the first month of a new year (8:13).

Here again, under the influence of Platonic philosophy, the classical theological approach to scripture followed the path of individualistic anthropology and misread the flood narrative along the same lines as it did the creation narrative. Just as classical theology viewed the creation narrative as being that of the "individual" Adam, it also read the flood narrative as dealing with the salvation of the "individual" Noah. However, a closer look at the latter narrative will show that the author's concern is still the same "earth" with which he was concerned in Genesis 1-4. The lesson of Genesis 6-8 is the following: due to the wickedness of Adam, "the man," the earth was threatened with obliteration, and it is only through the righteousness of Noah, "the son of man (Adam)," that God will condescend to salvage the earth he created with its inhabitants, vegetation as well as animals and humans.

---

[10] From the same root as *noah* and *nuh*.

That the earth, including the life it supports, is the subject matter throughout the flood story is evident from the following recurring features:

1. Not only does the initial decision affect the earth and its "inhabitants" (6:7, 17), but repeatedly God's concern is that the ark is to protect all living breath (6:19-21; 7:2-3, 8-9, 14-16; 8:17, 19, 21).[11] Even the covenant is inclusive of the animals (9:10, 12, 15-16)!

2. The last statement after the restoration is a reversal of the initial decision and thus concerns the earth, not man: "While the earth remains, seedtime and harvest, cold and heat, summer and winter, day and night, shall not cease." (8:22) It is this promise that will secure the continued life of vegetation and, through it, of man and animal, as was originally the case (1:29-30) when "God saw everything that he had made, and behold, it was very good" (v.31). The same concern at the post-diluvial restoration is iterated in conjunction with the covenant: "I set my bow in the cloud, and it shall be a sign of the covenant *between me and the earth*. When I bring clouds over *the earth* and the bow is seen in the clouds…" (9:13-14). It is only then that the "earth" is, as it were, expanded to include all life on it; still, it is the repeated mention of the "earth" that steals the show: "'I will remember my covenant which is between me and you and every living creature of all flesh; and the waters shall never again become a flood to destroy all flesh. When the bow is in the clouds, I will look upon it and remember

---

[11] Actually and ironically, Noah needed the crow and the dove to establish the viability of the ground for him and his family.

the everlasting covenant between God and every living creature of all flesh that is *upon the earth.*' God said to Noah, 'This is the sign of the covenant which I have established between me and all flesh that is *upon the earth.*'" (vv.15-17)

Even if one overlooks the striking overarching centrality of the earth, still one is not entitled to read the flood narrative anthropologically since, together with Noah, the animals as well as his sons and their wives are systematically included in the process of God's plan of restoration. Here again, the first statement after the restoration is: "And God blessed Noah and his sons, and said to them, 'Be fruitful and multiply, and fill the earth... And you, be fruitful and multiply, bring forth abundantly on the earth and multiply in it.'" (9:1 and 7) This corresponds to the blessing bestowed earlier upon the animals: "Bring forth with you every living thing that is with you of all flesh—birds and animals and every creeping thing that creeps on the earth—that they may breed abundantly on the earth, and be fruitful and multiply upon the earth." (8:17) As we saw in Genesis 1, the purview of the divine blessing is procreation and thus "the man in the image of God" (9:6) is always "male and female" (1:27; 5:2). And this human community is not an aggregation of self-standing Platonic "souls," but rather a community of bodies which needs to be nurtured by the fruit of the earth (1:29) just as the animals are (v.30) since both are "flesh upon the earth" (9:15-17).

However, the human being is to recognize in thanksgiving that all life on earth is anchored in God's blessing bestowed through the "seed" of procreation, whether agricultural or animal. This thanksgiving the human being renders by offering to God the "first fruits" (*bekor*) of that seed, which will be required by the Law, as we shall see later.[12] Here also, the same requirement was made by God himself as is evident from that Noah was asked to take with him "seven pairs of all clean animals, the male and his mate… and seven pairs of the birds of the air also, male and female" (7:2-3) with the view of securing the supply of burnt offerings after the restoration of the earth:

> So Noah went forth, and his sons and his wife and his sons' wives with him. And every beast, every creeping thing, and every bird, everything that moves upon the earth, went forth by families out of the ark. Then Noah built an altar to the Lord, and took of every clean animal and of every clean bird, and offered burnt offerings on the altar. And when the Lord smelled the pleasing odor, the Lord said in his heart, "I will never again curse the ground because of man, for the imagination of man's heart is evil from his youth; neither will I ever again destroy every living creature as I have done. While the earth remains, seedtime and harvest, cold and heat, summer and winter, day and night, shall not cease." (8:18-22)

The Covenant

The end of Noah's *toledot* is richer and more complex than meets the eye. The first part deals with the Noachic covenant (9:1-17). Just as in the case of the later Davidic covenant, God's commitment is unilateral, which makes it an act of grace. By the same token, again as in the case of David, it entails a test on God's part to see if the recipient will abide in that "grace." Indeed, before the establishment of the covenant (9:8) which was promised earlier (6:18), God makes a concession that goes against his original will of having the human beings share with

---

[12] See e.g. Ex 23:16; 34:22; Lev 2:12, 14; 23:10 17, 20.

the animals the fruit of the earth as well as satisfy themselves with it (1:28-29):

> The fear of you and the dread of you shall be upon every beast of the earth, and upon every bird of the air, upon everything that creeps on the ground and all the fish of the sea; into your hand they are delivered. Every moving thing that lives shall be food for you; and as I gave you the green plants, I give you everything. Only you shall not eat flesh with its life, that is, its blood. For your lifeblood I will surely require a reckoning; of every beast I will require it and of man. (9:2-5)

This concession of killing animals had already been heralded in the text that spoke of garments of skins (3:21).[13] However, it was God who clothed the human beings with such and here, we are told, he keeps that prerogative. Any animal life, expressed through blood and breathing,[14] is his, and only his, to take as well as give. Hence, in keeping with this, one is to let the animal blood flow out of its body before consuming the flesh. Consequently, if animals are for food, they are not for killing at will. The latter is considered as much a murder as the killing of man is since, in both cases, the sign of life is the "breath" (*nepheš*) granted by God. This reality is underscored to the extreme in Ecclesiastes where we are told that "they both have the same spirit (*ruah*)" (3:19). The last statement need not be perceived as scandalous since the overlapping in meaning between "breath" and "spirit" is already present in the first chapters of Genesis. The "breath (*nešamah*; breeze) of life" that "God breathed into the nostrils of man" (2:7) is encountered as the "breath

---

[13] See my comments earlier.
[14] Even nowadays the breathing and the pulse (blood flowing in the veins) are considered the basic signs of life

(*nešamah*; breeze) of the spirit (*ruah*) of life" (7:22) and, for short, the "spirit of life" (7:15) with reference to the animals.[15]

This bridling of the killing at will is clearly an anti-kingly statement. Indeed, when it comes to the killing of (the) man by (the) man, we are referred back to the statement that the man was made in the image of God (9:6). Traditionally, being in the image of God is read as applying to the man who is killed. However, this does not make any sense since the seriousness of killing another man has been taken care of in the preceding verse where it is God himself who enforces the punishment: "Of every man's brother *I will require the life of man*." (v.5) Consequently, the additional v.6 indicates that the representative of God in this matter is any man assigned to the position of judge on behalf of God, as prescribed in the Mosaic law, which was issued when there was no king.[16] The corollary is that the king himself, who later will occupy the throne of judgment, is accountable to that Law and is not above it as Deuteronomy will assert (17:18-20) and as Elijah will later make clear to King Ahab (1 Kg 21:17-19).

The Shaming of Noah

After God has salvaged his earth and unilaterally committed himself to preserving it in spite of man's disobedience, the author finishes Noah's *toledot* with a story showing that man's fate of either blessing or curse on that same earth is of his own doing. This teaching is none else than the one that will be presented to Israel upon its entry into Canaan (Lev 26; Deut 28) after having been salvaged from the flooding waters of the Sea of

---

[15] Again the overlapping in meaning between *nešamah* (breeze; breath) and *ruah* (spirit) is evident in the phrase *ruah hayyom* (spirit [cool breeze] of the day) in Gen 3:8: "And they heard the sound of the Lord God walking in the garden in the *cool of the day*."

[16] Lev 24:17; Num 35:9-34.

Reeds.[17] This intention on the author's part is evident in the way the curse aimed at Ham actually hit his son, Canaan (9:22, 25).

Actually, this story of the shaming of Noah is scripturally programmatic as well as overarching. It follows the same vein we encountered in the creation and flood narratives. The prophetic view and terminology that informed the Mosaic law is made to apply to the entire humanity since both the prophetic teaching and the Law have ultimately "the man" in view:

> He has showed you, O man (*'adam*), what is good; and what does the Lord require of you but to do justice, and to love kindness, and to walk humbly with your God? (Mic 6:8)

> All the commandment which I command you this day you shall be careful to do, that you may live and multiply, and go in and inherit the earth which the Lord swore to give to your fathers. And you shall remember all the way which the Lord your God has led you these forty years in the wilderness, that he might humble you, testing you to know what was in your heart, whether you would keep his commandments, or not. And he humbled you and let you hunger and fed you with manna, which you did not know, nor did your fathers know; that he might make you know that (the) man (*ha'adam*) does not live by bread alone, but that (the) man (*ha'adam*) lives by everything that proceeds out of the mouth of the Lord. (Deut 8:1-3)

In the passage from Deuteronomy, the parallelism with Noah is striking. Both Israel and Noah are tested as to whether they would abide by God's commandments in the "new" earth that was just granted to them to live on. However, in the story of

---

[17] In turn, this corroborates my earlier reading in conjunction with the *tebah* (ark) where I indicated that the mention of "reeds" looked beyond a connection between Noah and Moses to one between Noah and Israel.

Noah and his sons, the test of obedience to God was made in
conjunction with one's behavior toward an elder. But this is
precisely, earlier in Deuteronomy, the topic of the first
Decalogue directive concerning the behavior toward the other
humans: "Honor your father and your mother, *as the Lord your
God commanded you*, in order that your days may be prolonged,
and that it may go well with you, in the land which the Lord
your God gives you." (Deut 5:16)[18] The seriousness of such test
is evident from the Hebrew *kabbed* translated as "honor"; it is
the same verb that means "glorify" when used with God as its
complement. Honoring one's elders is tantamount to honoring
God, the ultimate parent. This is the well known Greek *evsebeia*
and Latin *pietas*, which is the required attitude of reverence
toward one's "seniors," be they gods, deceased, or elders. The
opposite, Greek *asebeia* or Latin *impietas*, is "wickedness," which
is despicable in scripture.

As usual, starting with Adam and all the way to Israel (Hos 2),
the reason behind human sin is the misuse and abuse of God's
gift to us, the earth that secures our living. After the disastrous
flood, Noah and his family were supposed to "enjoy a life of rest
(*nuah*)" on the covenanted earth. The vineyard and its fruit, the
wine, is a sign of such life of rest and enjoyment: "Noah was the
first tiller of the soil. He planted a vineyard; and he drank of the
wine." (Gen 9:20-21a). However, he "became drunk, and lay
uncovered in his tent" (v.21b). Thus, it is Noah's abuse that
prompted Ham's temptation.[19]

---

[18] See also Ex 20:12 (Honor your father and your mother in order that your days may
be long in the land which the Lord your God gives you).
[19] One is not to be perplexed at Noah's imperfection. Later, even Abraham himself will
show signs of such.

Just as Noah's name is functional so are the names of his children. The first, *šem*, means "name," and thus "fame" as in "to make a name for oneself."[20] It fits perfectly the patriarch whose progeny will include Abraham "by whom all the families of the earth shall bless themselves" (Gen 12:3). The second, *ham*, is from the same root as "heat" and thus "ire." He, or at least his descendant Canaan, incurs the divine wrath and curse. The explanation of Jepheth (*yephet*)[21] is more complex.[22] The solution, however, is to be found in Noah's statement concerning him, as was the case with his brothers. "God enlarge (open up) Jepheth" (Gen 9:27) sounds thus in Hebrew: *yapht 'elohim leyephet*. The correspondence between the verb "open" and the personal name is unmistakable. Whereas Ham is cursed and Shem is blessed, Jepheth is neither blessed nor cursed; he simply shares in his brother's blessing:

> When Noah awoke from his wine and knew what his youngest son had done to him, he said, "Cursed be Canaan; a slave of slaves shall he be to his brothers." He also said, "Blessed by the Lord my God be Shem; and let Canaan be his slave. God enlarge Jepheth, and let him dwell in the tents of Shem; and let Canaan be his slave." (9:24-27)

The reason for that will become clear in the *toledot* of Noah's sons (Gen 10).

---

[20] See e.g. Gen 11:14; 12:2; Ps 72:17-19.

[21] As in the case of Lemech/Lamech (see ch.1 n.61) Jepheth is to be preferred over Japheth, for the same reason. Actually, the Hebrew *yephet* occurs in Gen 7:13; 9:23, 27; 10:2, 21; and 1 Chr 1:5.

[22] I am dismissing the consideration that it would be from the root *yapheh* (beautiful) for three reasons. The first is that such explanation does not fit the fate of Jepheth in the same way as with Shem and Ham. Secondly, one would have expected the straightforward *yapheh* instead of the convoluted *yephet*. The third and most compelling reason is the one I discuss in the body of the text.

The Peoples of the Earth

Scripture is adamant about the oneness of the human race. Just
as the pre-diluvial humanity is Adamic, the post-diluvial human
race stems from Noah. In the latter case the oneness is further
underscored in that we are presented with the *toledot* of the three
children together:[23] "These are the *toledot* of *the sons of Noah*,
Shem, Ham, and Japheth." (Gen 10:1a) The addition "and were
born to them (these just mentioned) sons after the flood" is to
anchor further this reality in the hearer's mind. And at the end,
after the three family trees, the author closes with the mention of
Noah: "These are the families of *the sons of Noah*, according to
their genealogies, in their nations; and from these the nations
spread abroad on the earth after the flood." (v.32)

The preferential tilt for Jepheth over Ham is detectable in the
phraseology used to speak of the spreading of their descendants.
Whereas the progeny of Jepheth is said to have spread out (from
the root *pharad*; v.5) just as the totality of the peoples did (v.32),
it uses the verb *phuṣ* (v.18) which has the negative connotation
of separate (from one another; scatter). This intended
connotation is evident in that it is this same verb *phuṣ* that
occurs later in Genesis 11. There the peoples planned to unite
"lest we be scattered abroad (*naphuṣ*) upon the face of the whole
earth" (v.4), and yet end up by being scattered by God himself as
a punishment: "Therefore its name was called Babel, because
there the Lord confused the language of all the earth; and from
there the Lord scattered them abroad (*hephiṣam*, from *phuṣ*) over
the face of all the earth." (v.9) The close link between the
progeny of Ham and the story of the tower of Babel is evident in

---

[23] The numeral 3 reflects assured totality (see ch.1 n.59 on numerical symbolism). The
toledot of Shem will be the subject of Gen 11:10-26.

the names used in both (Shinar and Babel) as well as the
reference to building of a majestic city:

> The sons of Ham: Cush, Egypt, Put, and Canaan. The sons of
> Cush: Seba, Havilah, Sabtah, Raamah, and Sabteca. The sons of
> Raamah: Sheba and Dedan. Cush became the father of Nimrod;
> he was the first on earth to be a mighty man. He was a mighty
> hunter before the Lord; therefore it is said, "Like Nimrod a mighty
> hunter before the Lord." The beginning of his kingdom was Babel,
> Erech, and Accad, all of them in the land of Shinar. From that
> land he went into Assyria, and built Nineveh, Rehoboth-Ir, Calah,
> and Resen between Nineveh and Calah; that is the great city.
> (10:6-12)

> Now the whole earth had one language and few words. And as
> men migrated from the east, they found a plain in the land of
> Shinar and settled there. And they said to one another, "Come, let
> us make bricks, and burn them thoroughly." And they had brick
> for stone, and bitumen for mortar. Then they said, "Come, let us
> build ourselves a city, and a tower with its top in the heavens, and
> let us make a name for ourselves, lest we be scattered abroad upon
> the face of the whole earth." And the Lord came down to see the
> city and the tower, which the sons of men had built. And the Lord
> said, "Behold, they are one people, and they have all one language;
> and this is only the beginning of what they will do; and nothing
> that they propose to do will now be impossible for them. Come,
> let us go down, and there confuse their language, that they may
> not understand one another's speech." So the Lord scattered them
> abroad from there over the face of all the earth, and they left off
> building the city. Therefore its name was called Babel, because
> there the Lord confused the language of all the earth; and from
> there the Lord scattered them abroad over the face of all the earth.
> (11:1-11)

Moreover, Nimrod, whose name is from the root *marad* (rebel), fits perfectly the attitude of the kings of Nineveh and Babylon, as well as that of the protagonists in the story of Genesis 11:1-9.

The artificiality of the names of Noah's sons is at its clearest in the way the author handles Ham's progeny. On the one hand, he blatantly includes under Ham names that should have been under either Jepheth, such as the Philistines (v.14) whom he links to Egypt (v.13), or Shem, such as Canaan and all those mentioned under him (vv.15-19) as well as Babel (v.10) and Nineveh (v.11) whom he links to Kush (v.8), which is Upper Egypt. On the other hand, he includes Elam (Persia) under Shem (v.22) instead of under Jepheth as he did the Medes (v.2). Finally, he names Havilah and Sheba under both Ham (v.7) and Shem (vv.27-28). Thus, when orchestrating his list of nations, the biblical author had two working references in mind. Firstly, the nations are lumped not only geographically, but also in spheres of influence. Secondly, the "enemies" of later Israel and Judah, which enemies will earn the divine "ire" in the prophetic books, are entered under Ham (*ham*; heat, ire). The corollary is that the areas of Ham and Shem overlap within the biblical scene of the Ancient Near East. The difference between them is not racial, but rather behavioral. Ham represents all the "wicked" who will be under divine ire and curse, and while Shem is a stand-in for all the "blessed" who abide by God's will and to whom God will give a "name" (*šem*; fame) as he will promise Abram the Shemite (Gen 12:1-3). As Jeremiah will make clear, not even fleshly circumcision will differentiate between Israel and the others, but rather circumcision of the heart: "Behold, the days are coming, says the Lord, when I will punish all those who are circumcised but yet uncircumcised—Egypt, Judah, Edom, the sons of Ammon, Moab, and all who dwell in the desert that cut the corners of their hair; for all these nations are uncircumcised, and all the house of Israel is uncircumcised in heart." (Jer 9:25-26)

How about Jepheth? He functions as representative of the "nations," that is, total outsiders who are not as such excluded, but ultimately invited to join in Shem's blessing: "God enlarge Jepheth, and let him dwell in the tents of Shem." (Gen 9:27). There are plenty of textual indications that militate for my reading. Jepheth, as totality, is said to have spread just as the totality of Noah's progeny: "*From these* (Jepheth's sons) *the coastland nations spread* [24] in their lands, each with his own language, by their families, in their nations" (v.5); "These are the families of the sons of Noah, according to their genealogies, in their nations; and *from these the nations spread* on the earth after the flood." (v.32) On the other hand, a closer look at the term *'iyyim* (coastlands; isles), encountered only here in v. 5 throughout the entire Pentateuch (*'iyye haggoyim*, the coastlands [isles] of the nations), will appear frequently in Isaiah and Ezekiel in reference to the (far) nations in contradistinction to Israel. Those *'iyyim* will one day be preached, together with Israel, the good news of salvation:

> Behold my servant, whom I uphold, my chosen, in whom my soul delights; I have put my Spirit upon him, he will bring forth justice to the nations. He will not cry or lift up his voice, or make it heard in the street; a bruised reed he will not break, and a dimly burning wick he will not quench; he will faithfully bring forth justice. He will not fail or be discouraged till he has established justice in the

---

[24] I am following the original Hebrew and even the Greek Septuagint in omitting the addition found in translations (such as RSV) that read: "From these the coastland peoples spread. *These are the sons of Japheth* in their lands, each with his own language, by their families, in their nations."

earth; and *the coastlands* wait for his law. Thus says God, the Lord, who created the heavens and stretched them out, who spread forth the earth and what comes from it, who gives breath to the people upon it and spirit to those who walk in it: "I am the Lord, I have called you in righteousness, I have taken you by the hand and kept you; I have given you as a covenant to the people, a light to the nations, to open the eyes that are blind, to bring out the prisoners from the dungeon, from the prison those who sit in darkness. I am the Lord, that is my name; my glory I give to no other, nor my praise to graven images. Behold, the former things have come to pass, and new things I now declare; before they spring forth I tell you of them." Sing to the Lord a new song, his praise from the end of the earth! Let the sea roar and all that fills it, *the coastlands* and their inhabitants. (Is 42:1-10)

Later, in Isaiah, we are told that the inhabitants of those far off coastland nations, the foreigners, will be granted a "name" (*šem*):

Let not *the foreigner* who has joined himself to the Lord say, "The Lord will surely separate me from his people"; and let not the eunuch say, "Behold, I am a dry tree." For thus says the Lord: "To the eunuchs who keep my sabbaths, who choose the things that please me and hold fast my covenant, I will give in my house and within my walls a monument and *a name* better than sons and daughters; I will give them an everlasting name which shall not be cut off. "And *the foreigners* who join themselves to the Lord, to minister to him, to love the name of the Lord, and to be his servants, every one who keeps the sabbath, and does not profane it, and holds fast my covenant—these I will bring to my holy mountain, and make them joyful in my house of prayer; their burnt offerings and their sacrifices will be accepted on my altar; for my house shall be called a house of prayer for all peoples. (Is 56:1-7)

And at the end of Isaiah we are told of the gathering of many nations in the new Jerusalem without differentiation between insider and foreigner. What is impressive, however, is that we hear, in conjunction with coastlands, the names of some Jephethite nations of Genesis. Notice the closeness in terminology:

> The sons of Japheth: Gomer, Magog, Madai, *Javan*, *Tubal*, Meshech, and Tiras. The sons of Gomer: Ashkenaz, Riphath, and Togarmah. The sons of *Javan*: Elishah, *Tarshish*, Kittim, and Dodanim. From these *the coastland nations* spread in their lands, each with his own language (tongue; *lašon*), by their families, in their nations. (Gen 10:2-5)

> For I know their works and their thoughts, and I am coming to gather *all nations* and tongues (*ľšonot*); and they shall come and shall see my glory, and I will set a sign among them. And from them I will send survivors to *the nations*, to *Tarshish*, Put, and Lud,[25] who draw the bow, to *Tubal* and *Javan*, to *the coastlands* afar off, that have not heard my fame or seen my glory; and they shall declare my glory among *the nations*. And they shall bring all your brethren from *all the nations* as an offering to the Lord, upon horses, and in chariots, and in litters, and upon mules, and upon dromedaries, to my holy mountain Jerusalem, says the Lord, just as the Israelites bring their cereal offering in a clean vessel to the house of the Lord. And some of them also I will take for priests and for Levites, says the Lord. (Is 66:18-21)

The Tower of Babel

Between the *toledot* of Noah's sons (Gen 10) and the *toledot* of Shem specifically (11:10-26) we have the episode of the tower of

---

[25] Notice the inclusion of the Hamite Put (Gen 10:6) and the Shemite Lud (v.22) as if the biblical author intended to include *all* nations in his purview.

Babel, which is linked to the previous passage through the term "language" (10:31 and 11:2). However, whereas in the table of nations the languages or tongues are many (10:5 and 31), the tower story starts with the one language and the same words: "Now the whole earth had one language and the same words."[26] (Gen 11:1) Since the end of this episode is the confusion of speech (11:7), the story functions as an appendix to the *toledot* of Noah's sons intending to explain the factual multiplicity of languages among the progeny of the originally one family.

Still, the explanation is scriptural; that is to say, from the scriptural perspective whose core is the critique of human arrogance, taking over the position of majesty and authority that befits God alone[27] is tantamount to rebellion. Consequently the story is woven around Babel (11:8), one the cities of Nimrod's kingdom or empire (10:10). Scripturally, as we saw time and again in discussing Genesis, the epitome of human arrogance lies in mishandled kingship, whether it is Pharaoh, or Solomon, or Sennacherib, or Nebuchadnezzar. Each is a Nimrod in his own way. That is why, scripturally, solely "The Lord is (the good and righteous) King." He alone is the fatherly shepherd who tends his (scattered) sheep as "one" flock, whereas the arrogant kings scatter them unto oblivion and death (Ezek 34; 37:15-28).

If I referred to Ezekiel, it is because the connection is in the similar terminology. The noun *biq'ah* translated as "plain" is the same that occurs in Ezekiel and there is translated as plain or valley. Its original meaning is "a (watery) spot in the open," and

---

[26] RSV Translates *debarim 'ahadim* into "few words," which does not make sense. The idea behind Gen 11:1 is to stress the oneness and the mutual understanding between the peoples of the entire earth, as a premise for God's "confusing their speech, that they may not understand one another's speech" (v.7).

[27] See e.g. Is 2.

thus is the opposite of a high and mighty summit. Ezekiel maintains that God in all his glory chose to appear to his prophet, not on the Mount of Jerusalem, but rather in a *biq'ah* (Ezek 3:22-23; 8:4), and it is in that same *biq'ah* that he chooses at the end to bring his people from the death of exile back into life (37:1-2).[28] Instead of just dwelling there, as Adam was settled in the garden of Eden and as Cain originally dwelt in the land of wandering,[29] they decided to build a city, just as Cain did. But they even surpassed Cain and planned to "build a tower with its top in the heavens" and "make a name (*šem*) for themselves." They disregarded the fact that the only valid city and tower are the ones that God erects as his vineyard (Is 5:1-2).[30] When the people "chip in" they mess it up (vv.3-4) as the Psalmist— ironically Solomon—asserts: "Unless the Lord builds the house, those who build it labor in vain. Unless the Lord watches over the city, the watchman stays awake in vain." (Ps 127:1)

God's intervention, as in Isaiah 5, was not to allow the human beings to realize *their* project. They wanted to build a city in order not to be scattered (Gen 11:4). God turns the table against them: "So *the Lord scattered them* abroad from there over the face of all the earth, and *they left off building the city*. Therefore its name was called Babel, because there the Lord confused the language of all the earth; and from there *the Lord scattered them* abroad over the face of all the earth." (vv.8-9) The repetition of the reference to the city as well as of the action of scattering intends to underscore that God *indeed* undid their doing, which "doing" had just been mentioned doubly in God's description of man's endeavor: "... and this is only the beginning of what *they*

---

[28] These are the only instances of *biq'ah* in Ezekiel.

[29] See my comments earlier on "land of Nod."

[30] In both Genesis and Isaiah we have the same noun *migdal* to speak of the tower.

will do; and nothing that they propose *to do* will now be impossible for them." (v.6) I would be remiss if I didn't point out the functional value of the verb *balal* which is usually translated as "confound." However, its most common meaning is "moisten." As such, it counteracts the action of building with bricks that have to be burned (with fire) thoroughly (v.3). It is as though the aim of *balal* is to extinguish the fire necessary to prepare the bricks. The irony is exquisite. Instead of burning the (already erected) cities with fire, as he usually does in the prophetic books, God here intervenes during the construction by not allowing man to fulfill his project of construction. My reading is further supported by that, until now, water rather than fire has been the medium of divine chastisement. However, since God committed himself not to use water as a destructive flood that would have engulfed men, he used it to stop the construction of their city and arrogant tower. By the same token, by "scattering" them (vv.8-9), he actually graciously preserved them in their initial calling, willed by God, of "spreading over the earth" (10:5, 32) in order to "fill it" (1:28; 9:1).

The toledot *of Shem*

The scriptural story line proceeds, after the flood, through Shem, and it does so without being affected by the flood which is presented, as I indicated earlier, as just a period within the lifespan of Noah and his sons who were born before the flood (5:32) and survived it (8:15). The author's intention to point out this "continuity" in the Adamic humanity created by God is evident in that the *toledot* of Shem (11:10-26) is patterned after that of Adam: (1) a person begets his firstborn at a certain age, then lives so many years during which he begets sons and daughters;[31] (2) in each case the genealogy ends with the last person engendering three children (5:32; 11:26). The difference lies in the point of reference, the creation of man in the case of Adam (5:1-2) and the flood in the case of Shem: "When Shem was a hundred years old, he became the father of Arpachshad *two years after the flood*." (11:10) The last phrase is meant to assert once more the transient nature of the catastrophic flood.

With Shem's *toledot* ends the story of the "beginnings of the heavens and (especially) the earth" which, in spite of man's misbehavior, God managed to salvage and keep. The *toledot* of Terah (11:27) starts the story of the "beginnings of the biblical Israel" who, when granted an earth to live on, will end up abusing it and thus forcing God's hand into intervening with another punishment unto instruction. At the end of that lengthy and detailed sad story, God will commit himself to another one-sided and unconditional covenant, the covenant of peace (Is 55), through which he will establish "the new heavens and the new earth" (66:22).

---

[31] Mention of the death and the total number of years is not necessary with Shem as it was with Adam (see my comments above).

Part II

The Patriarchal Narratives

3

Overview of Genesis 11-36

Now that the covenant is introduced as binding on God in his gracefulness and on all human beings in their obedience to him, scripture moves in another direction to show how man keeps contravening this expectation of obedience. The story of Jacob, one descendant of Noah, is used as an exemplar of man's continuing disobedience in spite of God's continuing gracefulness. This is so much the case that the readers of the scriptural text are to view themselves as part of the biblical Israel.[1] This is not just a matter of necessary literary fiction; it is imposed by the biblical literature itself since it presents the story of Jacob *along the same lines* as the stories of Adam and Noah. The stories of Adam and Noah shape the presentation of the subsequent expanded biblical stories of Jacob and his progeny between Genesis 25:19 and 2 Kings 25:30. So just as the narratives of Adam and Noah contain the entire thesis of scripture, the overarching patriarchal narratives do the same, only in more detail.

The questions that then arise are: "Why include stories of Abraham and Isaac and not just those of Jacob?" "Why is the transition to the main character of the biblical story made via both Abraham and Isaac—why not via only one of the two?" In order to answer these questions, let me begin by pointing out the

---

[1] In the same way as, for example, the hearer of the Book of Proverbs has to assume that he is the "son" and the "disciple" referred to in that book, and the hearers of Paul's message to the Corinthians have to assume the role of being themselves those Corinthians.

obvious strong parallelism between Abraham and Jacob, with Isaac functioning as "bridge" between the other two. In the biblical text, the main bulk of the information connected with Isaac deals with him as the son of Abraham (his birth and potential sacrifice), or as the father of Jacob (the rather lengthy story of his marriage, the blessing of Jacob rather than Esau). The only exception is his dealings with Abimelech, which will be discussed later. As for Abraham and Jacob, their stories are much more "substantial." One can, so to speak, "make a movie" of either without much of a role for Isaac. An "Isaac movie," however, cannot be done without a starring role for either Abraham or Jacob.

It is also important to point out that the stories of all three forefathers, Abraham, Isaac, and Jacob, have one feature in common and that is God's underlying interest in the entire humanity. Just as God had in his purview *all* the descendants of Adam and *all* the descendants of Noah, so also here in the patriarchal narratives he cares for *all* the descendants of Abraham. Just as with Noah where care is taken to account for the genealogy of all three of his children, so also here in the patriarchal narratives we are appraised in detail of the fate of the progeny of Ishmael and Esau. In the same statement in which God speaks of his covenant with the not yet born Isaac, he promises to care for Ishmael by making him a full people of twelve tribes:

> No, but Sarah your wife shall bear you a son, and you shall call his name Isaac. I will establish my covenant with him as an everlasting covenant for his descendants after him. As for Ishmael, I have heard you; behold, *I will bless him and make him fruitful and multiply him exceedingly; he shall be the father of twelve princes, and I will make him a great nation.* But I will establish my covenant

with Isaac, whom Sarah shall bear to you at this season next year. (17:19-21)

Not only are Ishmael's descendants accounted for one by one, but we are also told that God allocates for them the earth of Havilah, which is watered by Pishon, one of the four rivers that flowed out of Eden:

> These are the descendants of Ishmael, Abraham's son, whom Hagar the Egyptian, Sarah's maid, bore to Abraham. These are the names of the sons of Ishmael, named in the order of their birth: Nebaioth, the first-born of Ishmael; and Kedar, Adbeel, Mibsam, Mishma, Dumah, Massa, Hadad, Tema, Jetur, Naphish, and Kedemah. *These are the sons of Ishmael and these are their names, by their villages and by their encampments, twelve princes according to their tribes.* (These are the years of the life of Ishmael, a hundred and thirty-seven years; he breathed his last and died, and was gathered to his kindred.) They dwelt from Havilah to Shur, which is opposite Egypt in the direction of Assyria; he settled over against all his people. (25:12-18)

The same goes for Esau, Jacob's brother. Both his progeny and his area of sojourn are accounted for in a full chapter (Gen 31) of 43 verses.

Looking more closely at the stories of the three main characters in the patriarchal narratives, one can see that all three stories actually fuse into one single narrative, if viewed from the perspective of the earth that is promised to them by God. Indeed, the narrative starts with "Now the Lord said to Abram, 'Go from your earth and your kindred and your father's house to the earth that I will show you'" (Gen 12:1) and ends with a reference to that same earth. This is so whether one considers either the conclusion of Genesis (And Joseph said to his brothers, "I am about to die; but God will visit you, and bring you up out

of this earth to the earth which he swore to Abraham, to Isaac,
and to Jacob;" 50:24) or the conclusion to the entire Pentateuch
(And the Lord said to him [Moses], "This is the earth of which I
swore to Abraham, to Isaac, and to Jacob, 'I will give it to your
descendants.' I have let you see it with your eyes, but you shall
not go over there;" Deut 34:4). The link between the end of
Genesis and that of Deuteronomy is that the entire Law, and the
statutes and commandments therein, is to be implemented
precisely *on that same earth*. And, as with the descendants of
Adam and Noah, Abraham's descendants, more specifically
Jacob and his progeny, will show that they did not hearken to
God's commands, and consequently they will be thrown out of
that earth (the end of 2 Kings), the realm that was given to them
as a chance to prove their loyalty to God.

The three patriarchs, however, act differently from the
perspective of their sojourns on the earth granted to them by
God. Abraham is born outside the earth of Canaan and dies in it.
Conversely, Jacob is born in Canaan but dies outside it, in
Egypt. Isaac is born in the earth of Canaan, *never leaves it*, and
dies in it. It is then this Isaac in whom God's will is realized and
only in him. Paul correctly understood this when he referred to
him as "the son [who came about] of the free woman [Sarah]
through [God's] promise" (Gal 4:23) and said to the Gentile
Galatians that if they are children (of God), then they are so as
"children of that (same) promise, after the manner of Isaac"
(v.28). Paul, the Jew (son of Israel), and they, the Gentiles, are
heirs inasmuch as they are "children" *the way Isaac is*. It is as
though Isaac has both what Abraham hopes for and Jacob keeps
reminiscing about. Yet when Jacob's descendants are again
granted that same earth, after a long exile in Egypt, rather than

behaving as Isaac did, they behave as their father did and end up losing that earth once again and are exiled to another Egypt.[2]

What is the reason behind this special handling of the patriarchal narratives? Before answering, let me recapitulate how scripture dealt with the story concerning humanity in general. The most striking feature of the story of humanity is unmistakably that scripture doubled it into two narratives: the Adamic story and the Noachic story. Man lost the perfect Eden due to his disobedience, yet despite this punishment, he persevered in his unruliness. God granted humanity another chance by restarting it through Noah, the obedient one. God even committed himself to a one-sided covenant. Through this covenant he relegated any full punishment until the end of times. At that time he will judge all humanity together and accept into his eternal "ark" only those who will have shown obedience as Noah did. Then he will establish forever his "new heavens and new earth," where the disobedient rebels will be cast out as in the days of Noah:

> For as the new heavens and the new earth which I will make shall remain before me, says the Lord; so shall your descendants and your name remain. From new moon to new moon, and from sabbath to sabbath, all flesh shall come to worship before me, says the Lord. And they shall go forth and look on the dead bodies of the men that have rebelled against me; for their worm shall not die, their fire shall not be quenched, and they shall be abhorrence to all flesh. (Is 66:22-24)

---

[2] See, e.g., Hos 9:3 where the exile to Assyria is likened to a return to Egypt: "They shall not remain in the land of the Lord; but Ephraim shall return to Egypt, and they shall eat unclean food in Assyria."

But according to his promise we wait for new heavens and a new earth in which righteousness dwells. Therefore, beloved, since you wait for these, be zealous to be found by him without spot or blemish, and at peace. (2 Pet 3:13-14)

As were the days of Noah, so will be the coming of the Son of man. For as in those days before the flood they were eating and drinking, marrying and giving in marriage, until the day when Noah entered the ark, and they did not know until the flood came and swept them all away, so will be the coming of the Son of man. Then two men will be in the field; one is taken and one is left. Two women will be grinding at the mill; one is taken and one is left. Watch therefore, for you do not know on what day your Lord is coming. (Mt 24:37-42)

For if God did not spare the ancient world, but preserved Noah, a herald of righteousness, with seven other persons, when he brought a flood upon the world of the ungodly... and if he rescued righteous Lot, greatly distressed by the licentiousness of the wicked... then the Lord knows how to rescue the godly from trial, and to keep the unrighteous under punishment until the day of judgment. (2 Pet 2:5, 7, 9)

Noah's descendants proved to be as wicked as his predecessors, if not actually worse in that they wanted to counteract God's plan of populating the entire earth. God foils their obstinate sedition in order to implement his original will: "Be fruitful and multiply, and *fill the earth* and subdue it; and *have dominion* over the fish of the sea and over the birds of the air and *over every living thing that moves upon the earth.*" (Gen 1:28) As if to underscore the seriousness as well as the solemnity of his decision, God issues this same command thrice to Noah: "Be fruitful and multiply upon the earth... Be fruitful and multiply, and fill the earth... And you, be fruitful and multiply, bring forth abundantly on the earth and multiply in it." (8:17; 9:1, 7) And, once again, after having spread humanity all over the earth

God concentrates on one exemplar in order to show that any human, living in any given location, would do exactly as the earliest Adamic community did. Thus, ultimately, he will be shown to be "justified in his sentence and blameless in his judgment" (Ps 51:4).

So this explains the extra care given to Israel as the biblical exemplar community, similar to that given to Adam. Just as Adam was set in a garden that was already planted and made fruitful by God, Israel is granted a good earth already "flowing with milk and honey." However, as in the case of Adam, the only condition required of Israel is to heed God's commandments:

> You shall therefore keep all the commandment which I command you this day, that you may be strong, and go in and inherit of the earth which you are going over to inherit, and that you may live long on the ground (*'adamah*) which the Lord swore to your fathers to give to them and to their descendants, an earth flowing with milk and honey. For the earth which you are entering to inherit of it is not like the earth of Egypt, from which you have come, where you sowed your seed and *watered* it with your feet, like a *garden* of vegetables; but the earth which you are going over to inherit is an earth of hills and valleys, which drinks water by the rain from heaven, an earth which the Lord your God cares for; the eyes of the Lord your God are always upon it, from the beginning of the year to the end of the year. And if you will obey my commandments which I command you this day, to love the Lord your God, and to serve him with all your heart and with all your soul, I will *give the rain* for your earth in its season, the early rain and the later rain, that you may gather in your grain and your wine and your oil. And I will give *grass in your fields* for your *beasts*, and you shall eat and be full. Take heed lest your heart be deceived, and you turn aside and serve other gods and worship

them, and the anger of the Lord be kindled against you, and he shut up the heavens, so that there be no rain, and the ground (*'adamah*) yield no fruit, and you perish quickly off the good earth which the Lord gives you. (Deut 11:8-17)

The intended parallelism in phraseology with Genesis 1-2 is unmistakable. The earth granted to Israel is not a possession; it is a trust. It is another ground and a garden for man to live on, sharing it with all other beings, human and animal alike. The difference, however, is that the commandment given to Israel, unlike that given to Adam, is within the confines of a covenant:

And now I am about to go the way of all the earth, and you know in your hearts and souls, all of you, that not one thing has failed of all the good things which the Lord your God promised concerning you; all have come to pass for you, not one of them has failed. But just as all the good things which the Lord your God promised concerning you have been fulfilled for you, so the Lord will bring upon you all the evil things, until he have destroyed you from off this good earth which the Lord your God has given you, if you transgress the covenant of the Lord your God, which he commanded you, and go and serve other gods and bow down to them. Then the anger of the Lord will be kindled against you, and you shall perish quickly from off the good earth which he has given to you. (Josh 23:14-16)

The word that came to Jeremiah from the Lord: "Hear the words of this covenant, and speak to the men of Judah and the inhabitants of Jerusalem. You shall say to them, Thus says the Lord, the God of Israel: Cursed be the man who does not heed the words of this covenant which I commanded your fathers when I brought them out of the earth of Egypt, from the iron furnace, saying, Listen to my voice, and do all that I command you. So shall you be my people, and I will be your God, that I may perform the oath which I swore to your fathers, to give them an earth flowing with milk and honey, as at this day... Hear the words of this covenant and do them. For I solemnly warned your fathers when I brought them up out of the earth of Egypt, warning them persistently, even to this day, saying, Obey my voice. Yet they did not obey or incline their ear, but every one walked in the stubbornness of his evil heart. Therefore I brought upon them all the words of this covenant, which I commanded them to do, but they did not." (Jer 11:1-8)

The covenant put Israel in a position similar to that of Noah, meaning that they were given a *second* chance. Indeed, the earth or ground that was granted to them was the same earth or ground in which they were born, yet they deserted it to go down to Egypt, the earth of their slavery.

Before discussing in detail Genesis 12-50, which forms the introduction to and the basis for the rest of scripture, both Old and New Testaments, let me sum up its most salient features:

1. Unlike any of the other descendants of Adam or Noah, the story of Jacob and his progeny is prefaced with a lengthy story of his origins. This story of origins includes that of the father and also of the grandfather. Moreover, it is the story of the grandfather, rather than that of the father, which is expanded. It is as though Jacob is the child of Abraham via Isaac. This is confirmed in the rest of the biblical story where the father of the "Israelites" is Abraham.

2. The importance of Isaac as the "bridge" between Abraham and Jacob lies in that the story of Abraham looks toward Isaac, and the story of Jacob looks back to him, especially from the perspective of the "earth" where Jacob sojourns. Put otherwise, Isaac enjoyed fully what

Abraham hoped for and what Jacob never fully enjoyed. Jacob and his "children" will always be, as Adam was, in the dilemma of choosing between the divine blessing and the divine curse in conjunction with their doing or neglecting to do God's commandments.

3. The importance of the previous feature can be seen in that, in the story of his origins, we have, in nutshell, the predicament of Jacob. Though "blessed," he ends up having to toil outside of his earth of birth in order to secure a progeny. And when he returns to this same earth, he is welcomed by his wronged brother, Esau. Still, Jacob squanders this opportunity by again leaving Canaan and ends his days in Egypt, the earth where his progeny will be enslaved for many centuries. Put succinctly, the dust of the "earth" from which he was taken and to which he was supposed to return keeps eluding him.

4. Abraham is indeed the "father" of Jacob in that Abraham's story reflects a life of vacillation similar to that of Jacob. This is important since, in the expanded story of Jacob, his descendants will land among the Chaldeans, which is where Abraham started. As we shall see, it is there that the same offer which was made to Abraham is made to Israel. This time around, however, there is a surer hope, for should Israel follow in the footsteps of Abraham, Isaac will be "ahead" of them as a beacon of light for them to follow.

4

The *toledot* of Terah

The traditional anthropocentric reading of scripture is dealt a hard, if not deadly, blow when it comes to the so-called "story of Abraham." We are used to speaking of the three "fathers," Abraham, Isaac and Jacob, as three subsequent individuals who followed one another in the ancestry of the scriptural Israel. We collect material about Abraham in the same way as we do with Isaac and Jacob, without giving consideration to the fact that, until Joseph, he is the only major figure who does not have a *toledot*. Terah, Abraham's father, has one (Gen 11:27) as do Ishmael (25:12), Esau (36:1, 9), Isaac (25:19) and Jacob (37:2). Abraham's personal "story," as it were, is part of that of Terah. Abraham does not stand out, as a hero character would, meaning that he is not a subject matter. He is rather a sub-character in the *toledot* of Terah, which is followed by those of Ishmael and Isaac. Thus, there has been throughout the centuries a misreading of the biblical Abraham, a misreading that would not have taken place had one heeded Paul's correct reading of Genesis in his letter to the churches of Galatia. There, Abraham is presented as (1) the father of the believers (those who put their trust) in God's promise (3:7), (2) the one whose offspring is Christ (3:16), (3) the husband of Sarah and Hagar (4:22), and (4) the father of Isaac who is the prototype for all believers (4:28). The term that links all those instances is "promise," and this is precisely how Abraham appears in Genesis, in function of the promise and thus of the future. Consequently, the author of Genesis opted for bereaving him of a *toledot*, a term which reflects one's existence through one's immediate progeny.

A correct—truly exegetical and not *eisegetical* [1]—reading of Genesis will thus have to consider Genesis 11:27-25:11, the *toledot* of Terah, as a unit and deal with it as such. It starts with Terah's begetting and ends, not with his own death, but with that of Abraham (25:7-11). This, in itself, ought not surprise us since, with the exception of Noah,[2] the previous sets of *toledot* did not necessarily span the life of an individual (Adam, Shem, Ham, Japheth). When Abraham is viewed as part of Terah's *toledot*, then one becomes receptive to the message of the text: Abraham's value lies in his being the link to Isaac in whom the promise made to Abraham is fulfilled. Since the hearers are the addressees and thus functionally Israel (Jacob), Isaac their father is presented to them as the perpetual challenge of perfection to be yearned for.

Abraham, Isaac, and Jacob

Still the question that remains to be answered is: "What is it that is promised to Abraham, fulfilled in Isaac, and sought after by Jacob and his descendants, Israel?" I indicated in my comments on Genesis 1-11 that God's subject of concern is the world he created, "the heavens and the earth." Since he rules in the heavens and his rule is perfect in its righteousness, the only

---

[1] Exegesis tries to get the meaning of the text on the basis of what it says, whereas *eisegesis* begins with a presupposition and tries to read it into the text.

[2] The reason is that, as I explained earlier, Noah's *toledot* is handled as a part of Adam's. The ending of Noah's *toledot* (After the flood Noah lived three hundred and fifty years. All the days of Noah were nine hundred and fifty years; and he died; Gen 9:28-29), which spans Gen 6:9-9:29, is the continuation of "After Noah was five hundred years old, Noah became the father of Shem, Ham, and Japheth" (5:32) which is a statement made within Adam's *toledot* (5:1-6:8). It is as though Noah's *toledot* is treated as an expansion of Adam's.

possible trouble can come from his earthly domain where man
has been appointed as his locum tenens. More specifically, as we
saw in the stories of Adam, Cain, and humanity before the flood,
the trouble comes from the locum tenens—the ruler himself.
After all, the earth is ruled by him (Gen 1:26, 28) and thus he is
accountable for the wickedness that is found on it. After the
blunders of Adam and Cain, the remainder of Adam's *toledot* was
given no less than 7295 years,[3] as well as Enoch's example to
follow, to show a sign of repentance, but to no avail (6:5-7). So
God struck the earth, but in his righteousness, he gave it—
vegetation, animal and man—a second chance, and allowed man
to spread from the area east of Eden (4:16) to the entire earth
(10:5, 20, 31, 32; 11:8-9).

Adam is a general case, yet the individualistic human being
does not seem to be convinced of this until he himself
experiences the general case. So, in order to prove that God is
"righteous in his judgments" (Ps 51:4) and thus give stubborn
humanity hope in him rather than in its own self-righteousness,
scripture zeroes in on one Shemite nation among the many
nations (Gen 10:1-32; 11:10-26) as a showcase. Again, and in
spite of the superlatively special care through the covenants of
circumcision and the Law, and after the lengthy story of no less
than eleven books and 2000 years,[4] Israel ends up vindicating
God's righteousness (Rom 3:9-18). And here again, when we
relinquish our anthropological self-centeredness, we realize that
in this story God is dealing with his chosen earth and all that
lives on it—vegetation, animal and man—which ends up cursed

---

[3] The sum of the life spans of Seth and his descendants up to the six hundredth year of
Noah when the flood started (Gen 7:6).
[4] The span of time, according to scripture, between Abraham and the fall of Jerusalem
at the Babylonians' hand in 587 B.C.

due to the disobedience of man, and more specifically due to God's locum tenens who, in this particular story, are the Israelites and the Judahites and, more specifically, their kings. If one keeps this in mind, then one will realize that the promise made to Abraham was a peaceful life on (one's) earth so long as one abides by God's will, as in the case of Isaac. Otherwise, as in the case of Jacob and his descendants, one's days on that earth are either shortened by death or ended by exile. And God's will, as we saw in the case of Cain, and as we shall see in the case of Israel, boils down to understanding that "the earth (any earth) is the Lord's and the fullness thereof, the world and those who dwell therein" (Ps 24:1; see also Deut 9:29). Thus it is to be shared, to our egocentric dismay, with the other "half of humanity," as in the case of Abel, not to mention the flora and fauna. God's concern with the earth and all that lives on it is what sustains the scriptural literary plot of the rest of Genesis. This is evident in the Lord's first words and overall intervention in the lengthy *toledot* of Terah (Gen 11:27-25:11):

> Go from *your earth* and your kindred and your father's house to *the earth* that I will show you. And I will make of you a great nation, and I will bless you, and make your name great, so that you will be a blessing. I will bless those who bless you, and him who curses you I will curse; and by you all the families of *the ground* shall bless themselves (shall be blessed). (Gen 12:1-3)

Furthermore, it is such reading of Genesis that will ultimately allow us to find the clue behind the author's intentional— though apparently enigmatic— omission of both Abraham's and Joseph's *toledot*.

The Early Story of Abram

Just as Noah's engendering his three sons is repeated at the beginning of his *toledot* (Gen 6:10) after its mention in Adam's (5:32), so is Terah's engendering of his three sons repeated at the beginning of his *toledot* (11:27) after its being mentioned at the end of Shem's (v.26). In the latter case, the repetition is more striking since it is done immediately and sounds redundant. It seems that the author could have dismissed its inclusion in v.27. However, a closer look at the context will show that, in each case, the mention is functional. In v.26, the hearer is surprised that Terah calls his second son after his father Nahor (v.24) and not his first son as Seth did (5:25-26)[5] and as would have been traditionally expected. Furthermore, he names his first son *'abram*, an exalted father, the assumption being that he would have many children and consequently Terah the progenitor would have secured forever a name (*šem*) for his ancestor Shem, just as men wanted to do in Genesis 11:1-4. Is there an intended link between Terah's arrogance and that of the men of Babel? I believe there is.

The story of the tower of Babel is at the end of Shem's genealogy (10:22-31), which is referred to as *toledot* in 10:1. Terah is the closer of Shem's *toledot* (11:10-26). Furthermore, Terah is living in Ur of the Chaldeans (v.28), a city in the vicinity of Babel. Thus, both the time frame and the geography are corresponding. On the other hand, the early part of Terah's *toledot* until his demise (vv.27-32) shows him as someone who continually does his own will. When Haran, Terah's youngest, bore a son before his two older brothers, instead of giving thanks to God, he followed in his father's footsteps by naming his son

---

[5] Both Adam and Enosh mean "man."

loṭ, meaning to enwrap, envelop and thus control. This may well be the reason intended by the author when he wrote that "Haran died (prematurely) before his father Terah" (v.28), presumably as a punishment by God for his arrogance. Yet, Terah did not heed the lesson and, instead of pushing toward the land of Canaan, he settled with Abram, Lot, and Sarai (from a root meaning prince, chieftain and thus leader of many) in an area called by the same name as his dead son Haran. It sounds as though he wanted to defy God by ensuring a legacy through the same means as the one taken away by God. In a few verses, the hearer will understand that God's intention for Terah's family was to leave "their earth" (12:1) for an earth of God's choosing. This is, I am convinced, what is reflected in another text relating to Terah's behavior: "Your fathers lived of old beyond the Euphrates, Terah, the father of Abraham and of Nahor; *and they served other gods.*" (Josh 24:2) Yet, the hearer is left with a divine touch of irony. Although Terah settles in Haran with the bearers of mighty names (Abram, Lot, and Sarai) that should ensure a great legacy, not only is Lot young and unmarried but the promising Sarai is ironically barren, not having had a child (v.30).[6] Since Nahor is not mentioned in Terah's company in Haran, the hearer is left with the thought that the only hope for Terah is that Lot, the son of his deceased son, would leave him a male legacy. The irony will be consummated when we later hear that the "encompassing" Lot was a citizen of Sodom (13:12), and he will beget only daughters who will lure him into lying with them to ensure a legacy (19:31-36)!

---

[6] The statement is interesting: "Now Sarai was barren; she had no child." It is as though the author did not want the hearer to be allowed the thought that Sarai could have had a child before she turned barren!

The turning point in this story is when God intervenes in order to counteract man's will and issues the verdict that the blessing, which I showed to be linked to progeny, will be secured to all the families of the ground ('*adamah*),[7] that is to say to every man ('*adam*), through Abram whose wife is barren. Only if Abram (the exalted father) relinquishes the earth he considers his, his birth kin and even his father's household, will God "glorify" his "name" (12:2), which is precisely what men were seeking to realize on their own (11:4). However, it is in Canaan that the real test is administered, the same test that will be Jacob's later in Genesis and the Israelites' starting with the Book of Joshua. Abram's first stop is at the oak of *moreh* (teacher) near Shechem among the Canaanites (12:6) with whom he will be invited to live according to the Lord's teaching (Law). He decides to build an altar (v.7) there, which recalls the building of the (temple) tower earlier (11:4). The second stop is Bethel (*bet-'el*; the house of God) where Abram is invited to realize that God's house is his household and is not something to be built; yet again Abram builds an altar to call on the name of the Lord (12:8). Earlier Enosh did the same without an altar (4:26). Still, the last test takes place in the Negeb (12:9). This is precisely when Abram fails, whereas Isaac will succeed. Abram's running down to Egypt at the occasion of a famine is a precursor of what will happen to Jacob. In both cases, God will be forced to intervene against the mighty Pharaoh to redress the wrong initiated by Abram's and Jacob's failure to understand that the solution to famine for bread is to listen to God's will, the true bread of life for them. God invited Abram and Jacob to settle in Canaan, and when tested, they contravened his will. Isaac, as we shall see, was preserved from such disobedience (26:1-6).

---

[7] And not "the earth" as RSV has it.

The story of Abram in Egypt (12:10-20) is one of three patriarchal stories (see also 20:1-18 and 26:7-11) that are literarily cast in what scholars refer to as "the ancestress in danger or jeopardy." It is as though our grandfather would tell us that his wife, our grandmother, would have ended as the wife of someone else before we were born. The outcome would be that we would not be who we are! Thus, the story is seen as a threat to our own being. This is, at best, very traumatic. Abram's lack of confidence in the Lord forced him to resort to a lie, and had the Lord not intervened to salvage the situation, in a manner foreshadowing that of his later intervention through Moses,[8] there would not have been any Jacob or Israel! The ultimate irony is that God's hand was forced to muster a great showdown with Pharaoh only to bring Abram back to where he was before this interlude, in the Negeb (13:1; compare with 12:9). The hearers cannot miss the irony of such an unnecessary, yet very costly, interlude to the extent that they would feel ashamed of their forebear.

Abram, Lot, and Melchizedek

The story of Abram and Lot (Gen 13) is, at a face value, a preamble to that of Genesis 14 where we hear of the abduction of Lot. It is a story of a friendly settlement of a dispute that could have divided brothers: Lot is referred to as the "brother"[9] of Abram in Genesis 14:8, which is the Semitic way to speak of even distant relatives. It is a generic term that is intended to tighten the bonds between those involved. As such, the story

---

[8] The parallelism between the two interventions can be seen in the use of the same noun *nega'* (plague) here in Gen 12:17 and in Ex 11:1 to describe God's last intervention against Pharaoh (Yet one plague more I will bring upon Pharaoh and upon Egypt; afterwards he will let you go hence).

[9] RSV has "kinsman."

looks ahead to the stories of Abraham and Isaac with Abimelech
in Genesis 20 and 26, where the two patriarchs are dealing with
a presumed enemy. Yet, in both cases, and especially in that of
Isaac as we shall see, peace is to be attained at all costs with a
presumed enemy just as with a "brother."

If Abram's descent to and return from Egypt in Genesis 12:1-
20 is a foreshadowing of Israel's sojourn in and exodus from
Egypt, then Genesis 14 is to be taken as completing the
scriptural story in order to make out of Abram a blueprint of
those who will be known as "the children of Ab(rah)am." After
abiding in Canaan, Israel and Judah, the children of Ab(rah)am,
are exiled into Mesopotamia due to the sin of Samaria and
especially Jerusalem, only to be promised another exodus from
there into God's new city, Zion (see especially the Book of
Isaiah). The parallelism in these events is evident from the choice
of terminology in Genesis 14:

1. All four foreign kings are from the larger area of
    Mesopotamia, the first being the king of Shinar and the
    last, the king of Goyim. Shinar has been earlier
    introduced as the area of Babel (10:10; 11:2, 9). Goyim,
    on the other hand, means "nations." In Isaiah and the
    other Prophets, the redeemed Israel is said to have been
    gathered from among the nations where earlier it has
    been scattered during the Babylonian exile.

2. The central figure among those four foreign rulers is the
    king of Elam (14:1, 4, 5, 9, 17). Elam is Medo-Persia,
    the land of Cyrus, through whom the Lord liberated his
    redeemed in Isaiah (44:28; 45:1).

3. Abram's pursuit reaches north of Damascus (Gen 14:15) which is the direction toward Mesopotamia and thus the exile (therefore I will take you into exile beyond Damascus; Am 5:27).

4. Upon his return from his journey during which he liberated Lot from the Mesopotamian kings, Abram meets "Melchizedek, king of Shalem," who "blesses him" (Gen 14:18, 19). Melchizedek means "(God) my King is (king of) righteousness" and Shalem reflects the state of healthy peace. The combination of these two terms is striking in that they recall the new Zion of the prophets, which is the city of God's peace based on his righteousness: "Let me hear what God the Lord will speak, for he will speak peace to his people, to his saints, to those who turn to him in their hearts… righteousness and peace will kiss each other." (Ps 85:8, 10)[10] Actually, according to Jeremiah, the name of the city itself is "The Lord is our righteousness" (23:6; 33:16).[11]

5. Melchizedek is presented as "priest of God Most High ('el 'elyon)" (Gen 14:18).[12] The concentration of the rare expression 'el 'elyon (God Most High)[13] in this passage is noticeable (4 times in the five verses 18-22). The adjective 'elyon reflects the universality of God as is clear from Psalm 82 where he judges all the other deities who

---

[10] See also Ps 122:7-9; 147:14 where peace is the main staple of God's city.

[11] See also Jer 31:23: "The Lord bless you, O habitation of righteousness, O holy hill!"

[12] That the king was also the high priest of the city in the Ancient Near East is evident in scripture in the story of the dedication of the temple of Jerusalem. It is Solomon who utters the prayer of dedication (1 Kg 8:14-53).

[13] It occurs elsewhere only in Ps 78:35.

are called *bene 'elyon* (sons of the Most High; v.6) and as such are under his "fatherly" authority.

6. The priest of this God Most High informs Abram of the realization of the promise made to him earlier whereby "all the families of the ground" shall witness that he is the blessed of God (Gen 12:2-3). Indeed the five "local" kings as well as the four "universal" kings have witnessed that God has granted him an impossible victory.

7. By accepting to tithe to Melchizedek as one would do to the temple, Abram acquiesces that Melchizedek's Shalem is indeed the city of God's abode, the new Zion. There, everything is given freely to everyone, without money: "Ho, every one who thirsts, come to the waters; and he who has no money, come, buy and eat! Come, buy wine and milk without money and without price." (Is 55:1) This explains the rather unexpected closing remark concerning Abram's refusal to take any money from the king of Sodom for the "good" he did him (Gen 14:22-24). The flow of the text between Abram's two encounters, with Melchizedek and with the king of Sodom, gives the impression that Abram's tithing to God lay in his having declined to accept a gift from the king of Sodom. In so doing, Abram acquiesced that his *yešu'ah* ("salvation" of the five ally kings as well as "victory" over the four adverse kings)[14] was actually God's doing, as much a gift from God as is the earth of Canaan which Abram had to share with Lot the Sodomite in Genesis 13.

---

[14] The Hebrew *yešu'ah* bears both connotations.

Abram's Trust

In Isaiah, the new Zion will be mother to many in a way incomprehensible to man. On the one hand, the city's children will be the expression of God's blessing:

> Look to Abraham your father and to Sarah who bore you; for when he was but one I called him, and I blessed him and made him many. For the Lord will comfort Zion; he will comfort all her waste places, and will make her wilderness like Eden, her desert like the garden of the Lord; joy and gladness will be found in her, thanksgiving and the voice of song. (Is 51:2-3)

On the other hand, that progeny will be totally God's doing since the city itself is "barren":

> Sing, O barren one, who did not bear; break forth into singing and cry aloud, you who have not been in travail! For the children of the desolate one will be more than the children of her that is married, says the Lord. Enlarge the place of your tent, and let the curtains of your habitations be stretched out; hold not back, lengthen your cords and strengthen your stakes. For you will spread abroad to the right and to the left, and your descendants will possess the nations and will people the desolate cities. Fear not, for you will not be ashamed; be not confounded, for you will not be put to shame; for you will forget the shame of your youth, and the reproach of your widowhood you will remember no more. For your Maker is your husband, the Lord of hosts is his name; and the Holy One of Israel is your Redeemer, the God of the whole earth he is called. For the Lord has called you like a wife forsaken and grieved in spirit, like a wife of youth when she is cast off, says your God. (Is 54:1-6)

Now that Abram has encountered the city of peace and righteousness (Gen 14), his test will lie in whether he will submit to this Isaianic perspective: although he does not have progeny to pass on inheritance (15:3), he is nevertheless to trust in God's word of promise that his progeny will be innumerable (v.5). He passes the test by believing God's promise, which makes him righteous (v.6), as Noah was (6:9), and thus he is the conduit through whom God will secure his promise of continual blessing, as he had done through Noah. And just as Noah did (8:20), Abram offers a sacrifice of thanksgiving to the Lord (15:7-17). And again, just as the Lord's response to Noah was the establishment of a covenant ((9:9-17), so is it with Abram (15:18-21). However, this covenant will not be articulated until Genesis 17 where circumcision will be the covenantal sign, just as the rainbow was the Noachic covenantal sign. The covenant of ch.15 is just a preamble to its consummation in ch.17. This is detectable in the deftness with which the author parallels Abram with Noah. Whereas Noah is both righteous and blameless in 6:9, Abram is merely righteous (15:6) and will be challenged to be blameless in 17:1.

Abram, Sarai, and Ishmael

In ch.16 Abram is tested as to whether he has truly accepted God's promise. And Abram shows that he, in fact, does not fully understand the promise. Instead of waiting trustfully for God to implement his promise, Abram accepts Sarai's proposal to realize the promise through their own human endeavors and, in so doing, forces God's hand. The story is belittling. Abram (the great father of many) and Sarai (the mighty princess) have to beg an Egyptian slave to help them in their quest to ensure a progeny that would seal their "might" (16:1-3). Moreover, their course of action ends up in blatant ingratitude: the jealous Sarai forces the pregnant Hagar away (v.6), an action that amounts to bringing her own hope to naught. It is, ironically, the Lord's counter action of mercy toward Hagar which proves to be the helping hand that brings to fruition Sarai's original plan (vv.7-15)! God who *hears* (which is the meaning of the Hebrew *yišma'e'l* [God hears]) Hagar's prayer in her affliction (v.11) *sees* her need and also *sees to* it (vv.13-14). He treats her with full attention equal to that he bestowed on Abram: "I will so greatly multiply your descendants that they cannot be numbered for multitude." (v.10; compare with 15:5) God even promises to protect Ishmael throughout the difficulties of his life (v.12), showing indeed that he is the Most High, the God of all. God's care for all is expressed in the covenant of circumcision; Ishmael is among its first recipients (17: 25), even before Isaac is born.

The Covenant of Circumcision

It is at this juncture, the birth of Ishmael (16:15-16), that the Lord challenges Abram to overcome his lack of trust by having accepted Sarai's proposal, and be "blameless" in his trust by "walking in God's presence," that is, according to his will (17:1). This challenge is articulated through his change of name and thus of destiny, which is the first such case in scripture: Abram is to be Abraham. Very often in scripture the name and its function are oxymoronic. The classic case is Paul. The great apostle to the nations has the Latin name *paulus*, meaning "little" (in stature and value). Moreover, this new name was to take the place of Saul, the namesake of the great first Benjaminite king of Israel, "a handsome young man; there was not a man among the people of Israel more handsome than he; from his shoulders upward he was taller than any of the people" (1 Sam 9:2). This explains the repeated boast of Paul when referring to his being of the tribe of Benjamin (Rom 11:1; 3:5). Here in Genesis we have a similar case of God's aggrandizing his elect by "humiliating" him. Abram, the mighty father of many, could not even have one child, whereas Abraham, the "father of the weakling sheep,"[15] is destined to become the father of many nations (Gen 17:4-6) and thus the one in whom God's promise (12:2-3) will be realized eventually.

> Behold, my covenant is with you, and you shall be the father of a multitude of nations. No longer shall your name be Abram, but your name shall be Abraham; for I have made you the father of a multitude of nations. I will make you exceedingly fruitful; and I will make nations of you, and kings shall come forth from you. (Gen 17:4-6)

This is in tune with Ezekiel 34 where the true king and father of his people is none other than the one who proves to be as good a shepherd as God: "I will seek the lost, and I will bring back the strayed, and I will bind up the crippled, and I will strengthen the weak, and the fat and the strong I will watch over; I will feed them in justice" (v.16).

The multitude of the progeny is a gift from God and not an expression of man's wealth or greatness. Just as the flock is the product of the shepherd without whom there would be only sheep scattered unto oblivion and death, so also in scripture God's children through Abraham are the product of his decision to adopt them at will. The willfulness of the divine adoption can be seen in that it includes equally anyone "whether born in your house, or bought with your money from any foreigner who is not of your offspring (*zera*', seed)" (Gen 17:12). Consequently, one is not born a child of the Abrahamic commonwealth; rather, one is adopted into it on the eighth day. That is to say, being a

---

[15] The Hebrew *'abram* is made out of the noun *'ab* (father) and the participle *ram* (high, elevated; thus haughty, arrogant). I consider the Hebrew *'abraham* to mean the father of the *raham*; the root *rhm* in Arabic, closely connected to Hebrew, refers to the sheep that is small in size, weakling. I owe this insight to an oral communication from Mr. Iskandar Abou-Chaar.

child of Abraham is not an entitlement at birth on the basis of DNA; it is offered as gift and remains such since a house "insider" who is not covenanted through circumcision "shall be cut off from his people; he has broken my covenant" (v.14).

Before moving to the actual act of circumcision where express mention is made of the circumcision of Abraham and Ishmael (vv.23-27), the author digresses to introduce Isaac in order to forego the hearer's assumption that Ishmael, "born according to the flesh,"[16] is the chosen one. At this juncture we hear something unique in scripture, the change of a woman's name: Sarai (my princes, my chieftains) becomes Sarah (one princess, one female chieftain). The function of this change is to lift the shame that was belittling Sarai: the one who is supposed to be remembered as the proud mother of many princes was in actuality "barren; she had no child" (11:30). Now she is slated to be a true princess: "I will bless her, and moreover I will give you a son by her; I will bless her, and she shall be a mother of nations; *kings of peoples shall come from her.*" (17:16) In that lay the test of Abraham: will he assume that the divine blessing ultimately needed his own procreation, Ishmael, who is about to be circumcised, or will he submit to the, humanly speaking, impossible proposition of God? And again, just as earlier in the case of the famine, he resorts to his own view of the matter and provides his own solution. He even ridicules God's proposal: "Then Abraham fell on his face and laughed (*wayyiṣḥaq*), and said to himself, 'Shall a child be born to a man who is a hundred years old? Shall Sarah, who is ninety years old, bear a child?' And Abraham said to God, 'O that Ishmael might live in thy sight!'" (vv.17-18) The original Hebrew actually turns the ridicule

---

[16] "Sarai, Abram's wife, took Hagar the Egyptian, her maid, and *gave her to Abram her husband as a wife. And he went in to Hagar*, and she conceived" (Gen 16:3-4).

against Abraham himself since *wayyiṣḥaq* also means "(and) Isaac!" Abraham will always be reminded through his son Isaac, a "thorn in his flesh," that the divine blessing will be realized through God's promise that Abraham ridiculed. Still, God's choosing of Isaac does not entail a dismissal of Ishmael, who will multiply exceedingly into a great nation of twelve tribes and will receive the blessing promised to "all the families of the earth" (v.20). The realization of this blessing will be enumerated further, together with that of Isaac, in ch.25 (v. 12-19). God is *'el 'elyon*, the God Most High and universal, who cares for each and all. The author's intention seems to be to remind the hearers of this reality when he ends God's conversation with Abraham with the words "God went up (*waya'al*) from (*me'al*) Abraham." Both the verb and the preposition entail the consonantal root *'l* found in *'elyon* and connoting "above, high."

Abraham, Lot, and the Fate of Sodom

The undergirding theme of the stories that follow is that of hosting the stranger. In that, both Abraham and Lot succeeded. They understood that, though granted to them, the earth of Canaan is still the property of the Lord who will command: "You shall not wrong a stranger or oppress him, for you were strangers in the land of Egypt" (Ex 22:21); "You shall not oppress a stranger; you know the heart of a stranger, for you were strangers in the land of Egypt." (23:9) These statements apply especially to Abraham who would not have settled in Canaan had the Lord not intervened on his behalf while in Egypt. However, the same Lord is the God of righteous judgment, and his earth is to reflect this reality. Consequently, the same stories function as a caveat to the Judahite hearers whose city Jerusalem is likened to Sodom by Isaiah (1:9-10; 3:9) and Jeremiah (23:14).

The Lord's visitation in Mamre proves to be a test for Sarah (Gen 18:9-15), which goes along with the testing of Abraham in the previous passages (17:15-33). Sarah fails the same test that Abraham failed: lack of trust in God's promise that their progeny will be the outcome of God's word and not of human (sexual) endeavor as was the case with Ishmael. The fact that both Abraham and Sarah ridiculed God's proposition and stood by this ridicule is corroborated in that scripture does not mention later that they had sexual intercourse the way it did with Abraham and Hagar (16:3-4). Indeed, scripture maintains the process of Isaac's birth between the Lord and Sarah. Abraham merely functions as a witness to that process:

> The Lord said to Abraham, "Why did Sarah laugh, and say, 'Shall I indeed bear a child, now that I am old?' Is anything too hard for the Lord? *At the appointed time I will return to you, in the spring,* and Sarah shall have a son." (18:13-14)

> The Lord visited Sarah *as he had said,* and the Lord did to Sarah *as he had spoken.* And Sarah conceived, and bore Abraham a son in his old age *at the time of which God had spoken to him.* Abraham called the name of his son who was born to him, whom Sarah bore him, Isaac. (21:1-3)

Later, Paul will point that out in his famous Galatians statement: "For it is written that Abraham had two sons, one by a slave and one by a free woman. But the son of the slave was *born according to the flesh,* the son of the free woman [was][17] *through promise.*" (4:22-23)

---

[17] The Greek purposely does not repeat the verb "was born."

In the following passage (Gen 18:16-33) Abraham questions the righteousness of the Lord's verdict regarding Sodom and Gomorrah. The lengthiness of the conversation between them is intended to show God's patience toward the arrogant self-righteousness of Abraham who wanted to outdo the Lord in matter of justice, if not mercy. The Lord honors Abraham by including him as a witness to his purpose. Abraham misunderstands this honor as being an entitlement to be part of the process. Later, Isaiah will fall in the same trap when he questions the Lord's harshness of verdict: "How long, O Lord?" (Is 6:11) The moral of the story is that God *is* just, by definition, as Paul asserts: "But if our wickedness serves to show the justice of God, what shall we say? That God is unjust to inflict wrath on us? I speak in a human way. By no means! For then how could God judge the world?" (Rom 3:5-6)

Genesis 19 makes clear that the actual unforgivable sin of the Sodomites is their lack of consideration toward the strangers as Abraham and even Lot have shown. It was Lot's *philoxenic* behavior that saved him and his family from Sodom's total extinction. Still God's mercy is not to be taken for granted. As can be seen from the case of Lot's wife, any disobedience of God's command on the part of the human being is condemnable. The story, in a way, is a repeat of Adam's contravention. The punishment was so harsh that, beyond the death of Lot's wife, the progeny of Lot was in jeopardy. The calamity was such that his daughters had to resort to incest, which is strictly forbidden in the Law, in order to secure a progeny for him and for them!

Abraham and Abimelech

The episode concerning Abraham and Abimelech is intended as a prelude to that between Isaac and the same Abimelech (Gen 26). This time, although Abraham was in southern Canaan, he had no reason to go down to Egypt: there is no mention of any famine. Still, what is more important is the name of the region he sojourned in, Gerar. This noun is from the root *gur* whence we have the noun *ger* meaning "stranger, resident alien, neighbor." In Hebrew, there is a pun: he sojourned in Gerar sounds *wayyagor bigrar* (he sojourned in Gerar [the land of sojourning]; 20:1). In this land where *everyone* is a sojourner (*ger*; stranger) God protects each and everyone. It is God who saw Abimelech's "blamelessness (*tam*) of heart" and preserved him from sinning (vv.5-6). Conversely, in fearing Abimelech, Abraham not only prejudged and misjudged Abimelech (v.11), but he actually showed lack of trust in God as he did earlier in the time of famine.

It is in Gerar, the land of sojourning and not of personal possession, that the promised Isaac is born (21:1-3). More importantly, he is the first to be circumcised "when he was eight days old, *as God had commanded*" (v.4). In order to understand correctly the following verses, one is to hear them in Hebrew since they are replete with a word play on the verb *ṣaḥaq* (laugh) from which is derived the name *yiṣḥaq* (Isaac);

> And Sarah said, "God has made laughter (*ṣeḥoq*) for me; every one who hears will laugh (*yiṣḥaq*) over me." And she said, "Who would have said to Abraham that Sarah would suckle children? Yet I have borne him a son in his old age." And the child grew, and was weaned; and Abraham made a great feast on the day that Isaac was weaned. But Sarah saw the son of Hagar the Egyptian, whom

she had borne to Abraham, playing with (*meṣaḥeq*; making fun of) her son Isaac. (vv.6-9)

Sarah was too much in a hurry to turn around God's *yiṣḥaq* from "ridicule (laugh at)" into "laugh with." She was proven wrong when Ishmael's behavior reminded her of its original meaning.[18] This brings back to mind the same kind of belittling from the pregnant Hagar (16:4), and she reacted with the same kind of anger she felt then. Consequently, we have a repeat story where Abraham has to care for Hagar, and God has to reassure him that Ishmael will not be forsaken: "And God was with the lad, and he grew up." (v.20) Once more, the Lord proves to be the God Most High, the universal God taking care of all those who live in his earth of Canaan. It is this divine behavior that prompts Abraham not to fear Abimelech nor even Phicol the commander of his army (v.22) and to make a covenant (of peace) with them (v.27). The covenant was sealed by an oath at Beer-sheba (well of the oath) before the Lord "the Everlasting God" (vv.33-34), which allowed Abraham to "sojourn many days in the land of the Philistines" (v.34) dwelling at Beer-sheba (22:19). The hearer of scripture is thus prepared to side later with the Lord in his criticism of the Israelites who opted for an earthly king, against God's injunction, out of (their misguided) fear of the Philistines (1 Sam 7-8).

Abraham's Sacrifice of Isaac

Only now is Abraham ready for the ultimate test for his trust in the Lord as the Everlasting God Most High. Notice how, although later in the story, multiple reference is made of "the Lord" (*yahweh*; 22:14-16), the passage begins with "(the) God"

---

[18] Actually *meṣaḥeq* is in the Hiphil form and means "make fun of."

(*ha'elohim*) testing Abraham (v.1). At the end of his series of failures to trust in God, Abraham passes the ultimate test showing he understood whose son Isaac was. Although Abraham had another son and will have more (25:1), he had to realize once and for all that his progeny was a gift from God to him, and not his as though it issued from him. The scriptural author points out this reality by not presenting a *toledot* of Abraham, as I indicated earlier. His only scripturally valid progeny is Isaac who came out of Sarah's womb *according to the divine promise*. That is why, in this chapter, Isaac is referred to thrice as *yaḥid* (unique; 22:2, 12, 16), not in the sense of "only"[19] but of "one of a kind." He is God's and God has all the rights over him; in this sense Isaac is a reflection of the Isaianic Servant of the Lord, who is his chosen one (42:1; 49.7), yet the one he decides to sacrifice (53:10). It is only in Genesis 22 that Abraham passes the test of trust in God, which was required from him in 15:1-6. That is why the promise made to him then that his descendants would number as the stars (15:5) is iterated again here (22:17). By the same token, also the blessing of Genesis 12:2-3 is repeated here (v.18a). And in both cases, it is Abraham's passing the test that secures the implementation of the blessing as well as the promise; indeed, God's last words are "because you have obeyed my voice" (v.18b).

The End of Abraham's Odyssey

Having fulfilled his function, Abraham exits the scene and from then on the scriptural text looks ahead toward Isaac and his future. Indeed, the last verses of Genesis 22 deal with the birth of Rebekah, Isaac's bride-to-be. Now that the progeny of her son is potentially secured, Sarah dies. This is an opportunity for the

---

[19] As in RSV.

writer to seal once and for all in the case of Abraham that the
earth of promise, and thus any earth, is not a possession, but
rather a gift from God to be enjoyed by all its dwellers: "The
earth is the Lord's and the fullness thereof, the world and those
who dwell therein." (Ps 24:1)

Abraham did not have a burial lot on the earth granted to him.
Such was offered to him as a gift by Ephron the Hittite who, like
Abraham, was a sojourner to the earth. Although Abraham
ended up by purchasing the gift (23:17-20), the legacy of
Ephron's magnanimity and his offer to share God's earth
remains in the story: "Isaac and Ishmael his sons buried him
[Abraham] in the cave of Machpelah, *in the field of Ephron the
son of Zohar the Hittite*, east of Mamre, the field which Abraham
purchased from the Hittites. There Abraham was buried, with
Sarah his wife." (25:9-10) Hearers of the Bible, especially
Abraham's progeny, are reminded that their forefather's burial
place will remain forever within the field of Ephron the Hittite.
Had the latter not been willing to give away or sell the cave,
Abraham would not have had a foothold in Canaan.

But, in order to comprehend the fullness of the message of this
pivotal story, it is necessary to delve further in the phraseology of
the original text. First of all, Ephron's property is referred to as a
"field," which is the same term used in Genesis 2-3 to speak of
the earth to which vegetation and animals are connected:

These are the generations of the heavens and the earth when they
were created. In the day that the Lord God made the earth and the
heavens, when no plant of the field was yet in the earth and no
herb of the field had yet sprung up, for the Lord God had not
caused it to rain upon the earth, and there was no man to till the
ground... So out of the ground the Lord God formed every beast

of the field and every bird of the air, and brought them to the man
to see what he would call them; and whatever the man called every
living creature, that was its name. The man gave names to all
cattle, and to the birds of the air, and to every beast of the field;
but for the man there was not found a helper fit for him. (Gen
2:4-5, 19-20)

Now the serpent was more subtle than all the beasts of the field
that the Lord God had made... The Lord God said to the serpent,
"Because you have done this, cursed are you above all cattle, and
above all the beasts of the field"...[20] And to Adam he said,
"Because you have listened to the voice of your wife, and have
eaten of the tree of which I commanded you, 'You shall not eat of
it,' cursed is the ground because of you; in toil you shall eat of it
all the days of your life; thorns and thistles it shall bring forth to
you; and you shall eat the plants of the field." (Gen 3:1, 14, 17-
18)

Between Genesis 2-3 and 23, "field" appears only once in the
story of Cain and Abel. Cain kills his "brother" while they were
in the field (4:8). The hearer of the scriptural text cannot miss
the connection. It is in the "field" that Ephron proved to be a
true "son of Adam," the true human being. He offered to a
stranger the field that Cain did not want to share with his own
brother.

One should add a corollary aspect to this point. The estranged
"brothers," Ishmael and Isaac, whom even Abraham was not able
to bring together during his lifetime, end up together in the field
transformed by Ephron's action: "Isaac and Ishmael his sons
buried him in the cave of Machpelah, in the field of Ephron the
son of Zohar the Hittite, east of Mamre, the field which
Abraham purchased from the Hittites." (25:9-10) It is as though

---

[20] The pun intended in the original lies in that "subtle" and "cursed" sound very close
in Hebrew, 'arur and 'arur respectively.

what Abraham was not able to do, Ephron's "humanity" brought to fruition. The linking of Ishmael and Isaac is further underscored in that at this precise juncture, at the same time and in the same terms, we are introduced to Ishmael's progeny and to Isaac's progeny: "These are the *toledot* of Ishmael, *Abraham's son*" (v.12); "These are the *toledot* of Isaac, *Abraham's son*." (v.19)

In Hebrew the name Ephron (*'ephron*) is from the same root as dust (*'aphar*) and the name Zohar (*ṣohar*) from a root (*ṣhr*) meaning yellowish-red, a color similar to the red alluded to in "ground" (*'adamah*) and in "man" (*'adam*). In Arabic the word *ṣa[k]hr*, which is from the same root *ṣ[k]hr*, means rock or a rocky earth. It is evident that the author wanted to convey the powerful message that Ephron's behavior is rooted in his correct conviction, consonant with the scriptural teaching, that as a human being, he is after all "dust from dust," and consequently "dust to dust." Such is Abraham too. In other words, there is no difference whatsoever between the two in that both share the same earth, whether living or dead.

In conjunction with this episode of Ephron the Hittite, one cannot help but recall Paul's assertion: "When Gentiles who have not the law do by nature what the law requires, they are a law to themselves, even though they do not have the law. They show that what the law requires is written on their hearts, while their conscience also bears witness and their conflicting thoughts accuse or perhaps excuse them on that day when, according to my gospel, God judges the secrets of men by Christ Jesus." (Rom 2:14-16)

5

Isaac and Jacob

The Marriage of Isaac and Rebekah

Genesis 24 is intended as the flipside of Jacob's arduous stay in Haran. In spite of the chapter's length, it does not compare with Jacob's endless trek (27:41-33:20). The intention is clear; Isaac, the true heir, stays at home while his bride is fetched for him by one his father's servants (slaves).[1] Jacob, on the other hand, will have to "toil, slave" (*'abad*) to secure his marriage and progeny. As mentioned in the introductory remarks to the patriarchal narratives, Isaac is the only patriarch who is born and dies in Canaan without ever leaving it. In spite of the tension between him and Ishmael, he is never driven out of Canaan as Jacob will be. Later, as we shall see, in spite of the difficulties with Abimelech's men, Isaac remains in Canaan. Thus, he is scripturally the true heir in whom God's promise is realized and, as such, functions as a challenge for Jacob and a "goal" for him to attain. Later, Paul will correctly read scripture when he writes that the true heirs and children of the promise are so "according to Isaac" (*kata Isaak* Gal 4:28).

Now that Isaac is married, Abraham's mission is accomplished, so to speak. There is nothing remaining for him except to join his wife Sarah "in the cave of Machpelah, in the field of Ephron the son of Zohar the Hittite, east of Mamre, the field which

---

[1] The Hebrew, just as the Greek, does not differentiate between servant and slave; they both use the same noun *'ebed* in Hebrew and *doulos* in Greek.

Abraham purchased from the Hittites" (Gen 25:9a-10).
Moreover, he is laid there by "Isaac and Ishmael his sons" (v.9a),
thus bringing the two brothers together after their long
separation due to Sarah's jealousy. That Ishmael is considered as
a full member of the Abrahamic family is evident in that, before
the detailed *toledot* of Isaac starting with Genesis 25:19, scripture
covers the *toledot* of Ishmael, the older brother, who had twelve
sons (vv.12-18), as many as Jacob will have.

The toledot *of Isaac*

The passage relating the birth of Esau and Jacob is introduced
before the episode concerning Isaac in Gerar and Beer-sheba.
This is done on purpose. The intention is twofold: to introduce,
in nutshell, Jacob's attitude and, concomitantly, to present Jacob
with an example of how he is supposed to act, that is, by
following in Isaac's footsteps. Early on the Bible introduces the
essential discrepancy between Isaac's attitude and that of Jacob.
Isaac understood that God's promise of blessing consisted in
fully sharing God's earth with the original inhabitants and the
new sojourner, and Isaac lived accordingly. Jacob and his
progeny will not do so.

The birth of Isaac's sons is worth analyzing in detail. The
entire story is intended to show how Jacob, unlike Isaac, usurps
the right of his brother in a specific part of God's earth.
However, let me first point out the difference between
Abraham's attitude and that of Isaac regarding progeny.
Abraham took in his own hands a solution to his wife's
barrenness. On the other hand, "Isaac prayed to the Lord for his
wife, because she was barren; and the Lord granted his prayer,
and Rebekah his wife conceived" (26:21). One sees here how
Isaac put his entire destiny in God's hands. However, man being

man, trouble was looming ahead even with Isaac's progeny: "The children struggled together within her; and she said, 'If it is thus, why do I live?' So she went to inquire of the Lord. And the Lord said to her, 'Two nations are in your womb, and two peoples, born of you, shall be divided; the one shall be stronger than the other, the elder shall serve the younger.'" (vv.22-23) One's attention is drawn to the fact that this statement on the Lord's part is not necessarily the expression of his will.[2] He is just relaying to Rebekah the truth of the matter.

Actually, Rebekah's predicament is similar to that of Eve with Cain and Abel, which shows that the story of Jacob is not so much a special story of a "chosen" people as it is a specific exemplar of the general story of humankind. The name Abel, in Hebrew *hebel,* means "breath, vapor" and thus something passing. The same noun is translated "vanity" in Ecclesiastes, from the Latin for "emptiness." The connotation is clear. Abel is representative of the human being whose life, however long, is after all like a passing breath: "The years of our life are threescore and ten, or even by reason of strength fourscore; yet their span is but toil and trouble; they are soon gone, and we fly away." (Ps 90:10) In the Jacob story, Esau functions in the same way. His qualities and behavior reflect that he is representative of man in general, the original inhabitant of the earth (of Canaan). We are told that he was both "the first" and "red" (*'admony*) (Gen 25: 25) from the same Hebrew root as "ground" (*'adamah*). Esau comes from the "field" and asks to calm his hunger with "the red, this red" (*ha'adom ha'adom hazzeh*). Notice the author's

---

[2] Point in case, for instance, is the Lord's allowing the people to have a king in Samuel's time although the decision was against his will (1 Sam 8). In that case, his intention was to show them how wrong they are and, consequently, to show himself just in his indictment and final verdict against them.

comment: "Therefore his name was called Edom." (v.30). The "red" Esau was referring to is nothing other than the product of the "ground" (*'adamah*), bread and lentils (v.34). However, instead of sharing the fruit of God's earth with his twin brother—the closest possible form of "brotherhood"—Jacob sells it for Esau's birthright (vv.32, 34), which is ultimately God's gift since he alone decides when to grant life.

Isaac and Abimelech

The first scriptural passage where Isaac promotes the story line concerns his dealings with the same Abimelech, King of the Philistines, with whom Abraham also had dealings. As in the case of Abraham, we are told that Isaac resided with Abimelech in Gerar. However the episode is intentionally more complex in that it links Isaac's sojourn with sojourns of Abraham, both in Egypt and in Gerar:

> Now there was a famine in the earth, besides the former famine that was in the days of Abraham. And Isaac went to Gerar, to Abimelech king of the Philistines. And the Lord appeared to him, and said, "Do not go down to Egypt; dwell in the earth of which I shall tell you. Sojourn (*gur*) in this earth, and I will be with you, and will bless you; for to you and to your descendants I will give all these earths, and I will fulfill the oath which I swore to Abraham your father. I will multiply your descendants as the stars of heaven, and will give to your descendants all these earths; and by your descendants all the nations of the earth shall bless themselves: because Abraham obeyed my voice and kept my charge, my commandments, my statutes, and my laws." (26:1-6)

The incident took place at Gerar, just as was the case with Abraham in Genesis 20:1-18, during a famine, just as was the case in Genesis 12:10 with Abraham. Isaac, however, was prevented from going down to Egypt by God himself and was summoned to dwell as a "sojourner" (resident alien) in the earth of Gerar (26:2-3, 6). In order to keep the blessing and the promise alive, Isaac had no choice but to obey since God's promise was phrased thus: "I will fulfill the oath which I swore to Abraham your father. I will multiply your descendants as the stars of heaven, and will give to your descendants all these earths; and by your descendants all the nations of the earth shall bless themselves: *because Abraham obeyed my voice and kept my charge, my commandments, my statutes, and my laws.*" (26:3-5) Earlier we learned that it is precisely because of Abraham's obedience that God's blessing and promise became effective (22:17-18).

Isaac learned the lesson and thus lived within the realm of the Law and its commandments and statutes governing the earth, and this is what will be conveyed to Israel: "And he (God) humbled you and let you hunger and fed you with manna, which you did not know, nor did your fathers know; that he might make you know that any human being (*ha'adam*) does not live by bread alone, but any human being (*ha'adam*) lives by *everything* that proceeds out of the mouth of the Lord." (Deut 8:3) Better, then, to dwell as a sojourner (that is, without possessing the land) in the location assigned by God's word (of command) and share it with the presumed enemy, rather than end up dying in slavery in a seemingly "friendly" land of plenty.

The remainder of the story of Isaac underscores his resilience in following God's command and remaining *as a sojourner* in the earth of Gerar, in spite of the repeated adversities with Abimelech's men, which Abraham himself did not experience. Just as in the case with Abraham, Isaac's story starts in Gerar (Gen 20:1-2; 26:1, 6, 17, 20) and ends up at Beer-sheba (Gen 21:14, 31-33; 26:23-33), the location of the covenant of peace with the presumed enemies. It is worth quoting the extensive passage:

> Then Abimelech went to him from Gerar with Ahuzzath his adviser and Phicol the commander of his army. Isaac said to them, "Why have you come to me, seeing that you hate me and have sent me away from you?" They said, "We see plainly that the Lord is with you; so we say, let there be *an oath between you and us*, and let us make *a covenant with you*, that you will do us no harm, just as we have not touched you and have done to you nothing but good and *have sent you away in peace*. You are now the blessed of the Lord." So he made them a feast, and they ate and drank. In the morning they rose early and took oath (*yiššabe'u*) with one another; and Isaac set them on their way, and *they departed from him in peace*. That same day Isaac's servants came and told him about the *well* (*be'er*) which they had dug, and said to him, "*We have found water*." He called it Shibah (*šib'ah*); therefore the name of the city is Beer-sheba (*be'er šeba'*) to this day. (26:26-33)

Notice throughout the play on the root meaning "take an oath" and how it is intimately connected with the root meaning "well (of water)." Notice also how the life-sustaining water is found only when the covenant of peace with the presumed enemy is consummated. Indeed the message in the story is clear: human beings do not live by bread or water, alone, but of *everything* that proceeds from God's mouth. Furthermore, ultimately it is obedience to God's will and sharing his earth with all others that secures his blessings.

The Stealing of the Blessing

Jacob's cunning was evident in the way he played on his brother's weakness in a time of need and stole from him the birth right (25:29-33). Here his cunning reaches new unthinkable heights when he plays on the weaknesses of his parents. He uses his mother's love for him and his father's near blindness to seal his act of stealing the irrevocable fatherly blessing (27:1-40). Both actions are actually sins against God's will: both birth and its timing is a divine decision; the act of blessing originates ultimately in God (Gen 1:22, 28). Put otherwise, Jacob treated as a right the divine gift. In doing so, he will be running after a happiness that will always prove elusive: having been born free in Canaan, he will die in Egypt, the "land of slavery." For all his apparent success, Jacob's action leads to the curse of centuries-long exile in Egypt for his progeny. Esau, ironically, remains in Canaan.

Jacob's Long Exile in Haran

Indeed, the beginning of Jacob's trek starts with the words "Jacob went out of Beer-sheba, and went toward Haran." This statement hints at exile. Beer-sheba was the residence of both Abraham and Isaac, the city of the peace covenanted with the Philistines, supposedly inimical strangers. Jacob leaves it in enmity with his own brother. The next time Beer-sheba is mentioned, it will be in conjunction with Jacob's leaving for Egypt (46:1-5), never to return from there except in a coffin (49:33-50:9).

Scripture tells us that Jacob gets a foretaste of his exile in Egypt while he is in Haran trying to secure a progeny for himself. Here again, one can see the discrepancy between Isaac and his son. Although both were to take a wife from Haran and not from Canaan, Isaac did not have to leave the earth of Canaan, let alone toil for his bride. Jacob had to work as a slave to Laban, the same man who acted graciously toward Isaac. Jacob got himself into this predicament the moment he decided not to share God's blessings and live in peace with those around him. Furthermore, his attitude when leaving Canaan is far from one of gratitude. To the God who vows to protect him by promising to be as much his God as he was that of Abraham and Isaac ("I am the Lord, the God of Abraham your father and the God of Isaac; the earth on which you lie I will give to you and to your descendants; and your descendants shall be like the dust of the earth, and you shall spread abroad to the west and to the east and to the north and to the south; and by you and your descendants shall all the families of the earth bless themselves. Behold, I am with you and will keep you wherever you go, and will bring you back to this land; for I will not leave you until I have done that of which I have spoken to you"; Gen 28:13-15) Jacob answers with a conditional vow: "*If* God will be with me, and will keep me in this way that I go, and will give me bread to eat and clothing to wear, so that I come again to my father's house in peace, then the Lord shall be my God, and this stone, which I have set up for a pillar, shall be God's house; and of all that thou givest me I will give the tenth to thee." (vv.20-22) Jacob's lack of trust is further compounded by naming the place of his encounter with the Lord Bethel (the house of God (v.19). He imagines that God needs a house when what God actually wants is that his will be done (Is 66:1-4; Jer 7:1-14). Jacob was merely trying to bribe God whereas Abraham understood that the true meaning of tithe was the care for the neighbor free of charge (14:20b-24).

The Marriage of Jacob and the Birth of his Children in Haran

The story of Jacob in Haran looks like a life of punishment for his earlier behavior. First, he had to slave (*'abad*) seven years for a wife to the same uncle Laban (29:15-21) who had no problem granting, without any condition, his sister Rebekah to Abraham's servant to be Isaac's wife. The culmination of the irony is that

Laban even fooled Jacob by giving him Leah instead of Rachel (vv.22-26), just as Jacob had fooled both his own brother and father. Jacob had to slave another seven years for Rachel (vv.27-30). Furthermore, although both were his legal wives, Jacob started an avalanche of family difficulties by preferring Rachel over Leah (v.30). However, "when the Lord saw that Leah was hated, he opened her womb; but Rachel was barren" (v.31) and Leah was fulfilled in having four children (vv.32-35). Two of these are Levi, the forefather of the priests (v.34), and Judah from whose loins came David the king who "will praise the Lord" (v.35).[3] This, in turn, stirred Rachel's jealousy (30:1) and "Jacob's anger was kindled against Rachel" the beloved one (v.2), which forced her to follow in Sarah's footsteps:

> Then she said, "Here is my maid Bilhah; go in to her, that she may bear upon my knees, and even I may have children through her." So she gave him her maid Bilhah as a wife; and Jacob went in to her. And Bilhah conceived and bore Jacob a son. (vv.3-5)

Her first son's name, Dan (v.4), is ominous: it is a Hebrew verb that means "judge." However, unlike *šaphaṭ* that has a neutral connotation of judging justly, *dan* usually connotes a judgment whose outcome is condemnation. The tribe of Dan will be "condemned" to relocate from an area near the tribe of Judah (Josh 19:40-48) to a new location outside the original area of the tribal allotments (Judg 18). Rachel's second son from her maid Bilhah is Naphtali (Gen 30:7-8). This name also has a negative connotation since it reflects the tortuous and strained relations between the two sisters.[4] This reading is corroborated in the

---

[3] The verb *hodah* (hiphil form of the root *ydh*) means "praise, laud."

[4] The root *niphtal* (niphal form of the root *phtl*) means "twist" and thus "wrestle." The derivative noun *phatil* is "cord" that is twisted. Consequently, *naphtulim* are the struggles during which one twists while wrestling. Gen 30:8 (Then Rachel said, "With

following verses 9-13 where Leah repays in kind by asking her
maid Zilpah to bear her two more sons to counter what Rachel
had done. The names Leah gives them reflect her gloating over
Rachel: Gad means "good fortune" and Asher, "blessed, happy."
The "struggle" between the two sisters continues when Leah
"wrestles out" through a deal with Rachel to have Jacob lie with
her (vv.14-16). The result is two more sons from her, whose
names reflect the fact that Leah "used" those two children as well
as Jacob for her own aims. Issachar is from the root *skr* that,
depending on the verbal form, means either "hire" or "work for
wages," which in turn explains Leah's statement "God has given
me my hire because I gave my maid to my husband" (v.18). The
following son Zebulon allows Leah to boast that, on her own,
she accounts for six of Jacob's progeny: "God has endowed me
with a good dowry; now my husband will honor me, because I
have borne him six sons" (v.20). Leah's "full" progeny
culminates with Dinah (v.21), a daughter whose name is from
the same root as Dan, the name of Rachel's first son through
Bilhah. Thus, Leah's boasting is checked by God who judges.

God stems Leah's boasting by granting the barren Rachel a son
of her own, Joseph. It is Rachel's son Joseph who will be the
protector of his brothers in Egypt in spite of the fact that he will
have been mistreated by them. The name *yoseph* comes from two
different verbs, *'asaph* and *yasaph*.[5] The first means "gather, take
away"; hence, "God has taken away my reproach" (v.23). The

---

mighty wrestlings I have wrestled with my sister, and have prevailed"; so she called his
name Naphtali) sounds thus in Hebrew: *wato'mer raḥel naphtule 'elohim niphtalti 'im
'aḥoti gam yakolti wattiqrah šemo naphtali.*
[5] *yasaph* accounts more readily for *yoseph*, the imperfect hiphil third person singular of
that verb; literally "may he add" or "he will add." *'asaph* is also defendable when one
takes into consideration that the consonant ʻ (ע) tends to be quiescent; thus "he said"
in Hebrew would be *yo'mer* (pronounced *yomer*) from the verb *'amar.*

second means "add"; hence, "May the Lord add to me another son!" (v.24) Rachel's prayer will be granted at the birth of her second son, Benjamin (35:17-18). Thus God proves again to be in control in spite of the human frailty of jealousy and arrogance.

Jacob's Painful and Inimical Stay in Haran

As mentioned earlier in conjunction with Isaac's marriage, the lengthy details concerning Jacob's stay in Haran—Laban's ruse on the wedding night, the tension between the two wives during their efforts to have children, Jacob's ruse to steal Laban's better flock (30:25-43), Jacob's fleeing from Laban (31:1-23), the difficult agreement between the two (vv.24-54)—is intended to enhance in the hearer' ears the contrast between the ease of the relation between Abraham's servant and Laban, on the one hand, and the arduousness of Laban's relation with Jacob his nephew, his own flesh and blood, on the other hand. In the story, hearers cannot miss the ambiguity in Jacob's appeal to God in order to solve his dilemmas. Twice we are told that he refers to God not only as the "the God of Abraham," but also as "the Terror [Fear] of Isaac" (vv. 42 and 53). Actually, even when Jacob calls on "the God of Abraham (his grandfather) and the God of Nahor (Abraham's brother and Laban's father)" to be the judge between him and his uncle, he nevertheless "swears by the Terror [Fear] of Isaac his father" (v.53). Jacob's lack of trust in God (28:13-22) has lingered within him through the years: instead of appealing to the fatherly care of the God of the promise, he prefers to secure this promise through fear that this God may instill in Jacob's opponents.

The Encounter between Esau and Jacob

This lack of trust is further depicted in Jacob's attitude upon his return from Haran. After having escaped all possible hardships, including a threat on his life, Jacob is still in "fear" of Esau (32:12). This is a double sin: besides the lack of trust in God, he considers Esau to be the same kind of person he is, vengeful. Esau, however, proves to be a true *'adam*, that is, a person who knows that the ground is to be shared with all other human beings, let alone a "twin brother:"

> Esau said, "What do you mean by all this company which I met?" Jacob answered, "To find favor in the sight of my lord." But Esau said, "I have enough, my brother; keep what you have for yourself." Jacob said, "No, I pray you, if I have found favor in your sight, then accept my present from my hand; for truly to see your face is like seeing the face of God, with such favor have you received me. Accept, I pray you, my gift that is brought to you, because God has dealt graciously with me, and because I have enough." Thus he urged him, and he took it. Then Esau said, "Let us journey on our way, and I will go before you." But Jacob said to him, "My lord knows that the children are frail, and that the flocks and herds giving suck are a care to me; and if they are overdriven for one day, all the flocks will die. Let my lord pass on before his servant, and I will lead on slowly, according to the pace of the cattle which are before me and according to the pace of the children, until I come to my lord in Seir." So Esau said, "Let me leave with you some of the men who are with me." But he said, "What need is there? Let me find favor in the sight of my lord." So Esau returned that day on his way to Seir. (33:8-16)

Not only does Esau receive Jacob warmly without asking anything in return, but actually offers to protect him further on the way! And Esau's offer is made to the one who stripped him of his birthright! In the text itself, God's judgment of shame on

Jacob is actually done through Esau's magnanimity. Notice how Jacob says: "for truly to see your face is like seeing the face of God, with such favor have you received me."

Just before the encounter with Esau, we have the episode describing the uneasy encounter between God and Jacob, where Jacob sees the face of God: "So Jacob called the name of the place Peniel, saying, 'For I have seen God face to face, and yet my life is preserved.' The sun rose upon him as he passed Penuel, limping because of his thigh." (32:30-31). Seeing God face to face, as Isaiah experienced, means facing Him as the judge (Is 6:1-5). Rather than punishment unto destruction, the magnanimous God opts for striking Jacob unto instruction through shame. Jacob will be limping the rest of his life, and he, as well as his progeny, will forever be reminded of the reason behind it: "Therefore to this day the Israelites do not eat the sinew of the hip which is upon the hollow of the thigh, because he touched the hollow of Jacob's thigh on the sinew of the hip." (Gen. 32:32) It is at this precise moment that we are told Jacob was presented with the graceful face of God through that of Esau: "And Jacob lifted up his eyes and looked, and behold, Esau was coming, and four hundred men with him." (33:1) However, the powerful Esau did not strike as God did, and Jacob got the message: he had better fear God rather than his presumed enemies. Indeed, in his recent own words to Laban, he refers to the Lord as the God of Abraham and the Fear of Isaac:

> These twenty years I have been in your house; I served you fourteen years for your two daughters, and six years for your flock, and you have changed my wages ten times. If the God of my father, the God of Abraham and the Fear of Isaac, had not been on my side, surely now you would have sent me away empty-handed.

God saw my affliction and the labor of my hands, and rebuked
you last night. (31:41-42)

The lesson is clear: the fear of God is to be applied to oneself,
not to the others, not even the presumed enemies!

The Continual Desecration of the Earth of Canaan

The rest of the story of Jacob and his progeny in Canaan is a
sad saga. The first incident describes the complete elimination of
the host residents of Shechem, using circumcision, the sign of
God's covenant, as a subterfuge. Shechem was Abraham's first
place of residence upon his arrival from Mesopotamia:

Abram passed through the earth to the place at Shechem, to the
oak of Moreh. At that time the Canaanites were in the earth. Then
the Lord appeared to Abram, and said, "To your descendants I
will give this earth." So he built there an altar to the Lord, who
had appeared to him. (12:6-7)

Shechem is also the first place of Jacob's residence upon his
return from the same Mesopotamia: "And Jacob came safely to
the city of Shechem, which is in the earth of Canaan, on his way
from Paddan-aram; and he camped before the city." (33:18) He
pitched his tent on "a portion of the *field* " (*helqat hassadeh*) he
purchased for a hundred pieces of money from the Canaanite
Hamor and his sons (v.19), just as his forebear Abraham bought
a burial cave in the *field* from Ephron the Hittite. Yet, it was
there that the unfathomable happened: a personal vendetta was
brought against a well-meaning neighbor who wanted to atone
in the most honorable way for his mistake.

In those times the rule in God's Law was: "If a man seduces a
virgin who is not betrothed, and lies with her, he shall give the
marriage present for her, and make her his wife" (Ex 22.16); "If a
man meets a virgin who is not betrothed, and seizes her and lies

with her, and they are found, then the man who lay with her shall give to the father of the young woman fifty shekels of silver, and she shall be his wife, because he has violated her; he may not put her away all his days." (Deut 22:28-29) In this story (Gen 34), Shechem, son of Hamor the Hivite, offered marriage to Dinah, the daughter of Jacob, after he seduced her. Before consenting to the marriage, Simeon and Levi, Jacob's sons through Leah, insisted upon circumcision for every male of the city. Three days after the males were circumcised Simeon and Levi entered the city, killed all of them, and plundered the city. Even Jacob was aghast and condemned their action, which threatened the very existence of his household: "Then Jacob said to Simeon and Levi, 'You have brought trouble on me by making me odious to the inhabitants of the earth, the Canaanites and the Perizzites; my numbers are few, and if they gather themselves against me and attack me, I shall be destroyed, both I and my household.'" (34:30)

The sin of Simeon and Levi is compounded by who they were: the second and third sons of the "hated" Leah, on whom God had mercy:

> When the Lord saw that Leah was hated, he opened her womb; but Rachel was barren. And Leah conceived and bore a son, and she called his name Reuben; for she said, 'Because the Lord has looked upon my affliction; surely now my husband will love me.' She conceived again and bore a son, and said, 'Because the Lord has heard that I am hated, he has given me this son also'; and she called his name Simeon. Again she conceived and bore a son, and said, 'Now this time my husband will be joined to me, because I have borne him three sons'; therefore his name was called Levi. (29:31-34)

The first of the two perpetrators, Simeon, is expressly connected to God through God's mercy to the one who is "hated;" yet, Simeon had no mercy. The second perpetrator is Levi, through whom the marriage bond between Jacob and Leah is secured; yet he did not give importance to the future of his own family. The name of their sister Dinah is from the Hebrew root *din* meaning "to judge, condemn." Consequently, the episode is ironical: those who decided to condemn others in the name of God, using God's own covenant of circumcision, end up condemned themselves. The ultimate expression of their sin is the use of circumcision, God's covenant of peace, to destroy their neighbors. In doing this they jeopardized their own future.

When God promised Abraham and Isaac to care for all those under the covenant of circumcision, he included Esau in his care, as well as Jacob (35:1-26). And just as Ishmael joined his brother Isaac at their father's burial, and information is given about his progeny (25:7-18), here also Jacob is joined by Esau at the burial of their father (35:27-28), and scripture gives full consideration to the progeny of Esau (Gen 36).

In contrast to the intolerant behavior of the sons of Jacob, God shows that he is the Merciful as well as the Almighty and cares equally for all the inhabitants of Canaan, in spite of their behavior. Again and again, he goes beyond the revolt of the human beings and cares for them for their own good, as only a true parent can and does.

6

The *toledot* of Jacob

The Joseph Cycle

It is precisely the point of caring for all that is conveyed in the
Joseph cycle, which is officially presented as "the *toledot*
(subsequent genealogy; subsequent story) of Jacob" (Gen 37:2).
This story revolves around two grave sins this "family"
committed in the earth of Canaan. The first sin is selling their
brother into slavery, an act strictly prohibited in the Law and by
the Prophets:

> When you buy a Hebrew slave, he shall serve six years, and in the
> seventh he shall go out free, for nothing. (Ex 21:2)

> And if your brother becomes poor beside you, and sells himself to
> you, you shall not make him serve as a slave: he shall be with you
> as a hired servant and as a sojourner. He shall serve with you until
> the year of the jubilee; then he shall go out from you, he and his
> children with him, and go back to his own family, and return to
> the possession of his fathers. For they are my servants, whom I
> brought forth out of the earth of Egypt; they shall not be sold as
> slaves. You shall not rule over him with harshness, but shall fear
> your God. (Lev 25:39-43)

> If your brother, a Hebrew man, or a Hebrew woman, is sold to
> you, he shall serve you six years, and in the seventh year you shall
> let him go free from you. And when you let him go free from you,
> you shall not let him go empty-handed; you shall furnish him
> liberally out of your flock, out of your threshing floor, and out of
> your wine press; as the Lord your God has blessed you, you shall
> give to him. You shall remember that you were a slave in the earth

173

of Egypt, and the Lord your God redeemed you; therefore I command you this today. (Deut 15:12-15)

This sin is again none other than that perpetrated in Israel according to the Prophets:

> The word of the Lord came to Jeremiah from the Lord: "Thus says the Lord, the God of Israel: I made a covenant with your fathers when I brought them out of the earth of Egypt, out of the house of bondage, saying, 'At the end of six years each of you must set free the fellow Hebrew who has been sold to you and has served you six years; you must set him free from your service.' But your fathers did not listen to me or incline their ears to me." (Jer 34:2-14)

> Thus says the Lord: "For three transgressions of Israel, and for four, I will not revoke the punishment; because they sell the righteous for silver, and the needy for a pair of shoes." (Am 2:6)

The second sin is seeking bread outside the earth that God considered adequate. Besides lack of trust, such amounts to putting bread on a higher level than the Lord's word of command, which actually assures us our livelihood: "And he humbled you and let you hunger and fed you with manna, which you did not know, nor did your fathers know; that he might make you know that man does not live by bread alone, but that man lives by everything that proceeds out of the mouth of the Lord." (Deut 8:3) At any rate, the children of Jacob had no excuse; they knew that Abraham went down to Egypt due to famine in Canaan and almost lost Sarah, their ancestress, and thus put in jeopardy their own existence! They also knew that Isaac heeded the lesson and refused to go down to Egypt; he remained in Canaan and put up with the scarcity of wells because he trusted in the Lord. With these two examples before them, the children of Jacob still opted to go down to Egypt, and were stuck there for four hundred and thirty years (Ex 12:40). They would have fared better had they accepted the famine as punishment for the sin of having sold one of their own into slavery.

But again God was faithful to his covenants with Noah and with Abraham and brought about salvation and forgiveness at the hands of Joseph, the wronged brother, the same way he did through Esau, another wronged brother. Joseph, whose name in Hebrew means "he (the Lord) will add," is the first son of Jacob's beloved wife, Rachel. She was barren and hoped for a son: "she called his name Joseph, saying, 'May the Lord add to me another son!'" (Gen 30:24) In reality, however, Joseph proved to be the one through whom God multiplied the people. As the father of Manasseh and Ephraim, Joseph ended up being represented by two tribes, the largest and most powerful tribes of Israel.

Joseph and Abraham

The story of Joseph resembles that of Abraham in that the value of both lies ahead. The promise to Abraham was fulfilled in Isaac, meaning that the ultimate value of Abraham lies in Isaac who came not from the womb, but rather from God's mouth. One notices a similar handling of the Joseph story. At the beginning, Joseph looks like someone with no future, not only in Canaan where, out of envy, he is thrown into a pit, but also in Egypt where, out of evil revenge, he is thrown into another pit, the jail. Yet, in both cases it is the intervention of divine providence that saves him, and he emerges as a blessing for Egypt as well as for his own people. One cannot help but recall God's promise to Abraham: "And I will make of you a great nation, and I will bless you, and make your name great, so that you will be a blessing. I will bless those who bless you, and him who curses you I will curse; and by you all the families of the ground shall bless themselves." (Gen 12:2-3) Also, as in the case of Abraham, his future is not so much linked to his biological progeny, but to what comes out of God's mouth. Of all the twelve sons of Jacob, Joseph will be the most blessed both by his father Jacob (Gen 49) and by Moses (Deut 33):

> Joseph is a fruitful bough, a fruitful bough by a spring; his branches run over the wall. The archers fiercely attacked him, shot at him, and harassed him sorely; yet his bow remained unmoved, his arms were made agile by the hands of the Mighty One of Jacob (by the name of the Shepherd, the Rock of Israel), by the God of your father who will help you, by God Almighty who will *bless* you with *blessings* of heaven above, *blessings* of the deep that couches beneath, *blessings* of the breasts and of the womb. The *blessings* of your father are mighty beyond the *blessings* of the eternal mountains, the bounties of the everlasting (*'olam*) hills; may they be on the head of Joseph, and on the brow of him who was separate from his brothers. (Gen 49:22-26)

> And of Joseph he said, "Blessed by the Lord be his earth, with the choicest gifts of heaven above, and of the deep that couches beneath, with the choicest fruits of the sun, and the rich yield of the months, with the finest produce of the ancient mountains, and the abundance of the everlasting (*'olam*) hills, with the best gifts of the earth and its fullness, and the favor of him that dwelt in the bush. Let these come upon the head of Joseph, and upon the crown of the head of him that is prince among his brothers. His firstling bull has majesty, and his horns are the horns of a wild ox; with them he shall push the peoples, all of them, to the ends of the earth; such are the ten thousands of Ephraim, and such are the thousands of Manasseh." (Deut 33:13-17)

If one looks closely at these two passages, one can see even more readily the importance and centrality of Joseph:

1. Although the testament of Jacob is one of blessing (All these are the twelve tribes of Israel; and this is what their father said to them as he *blessed* them, *blessing* each with the *blessing* suitable to him; Gen 49:28), the term "blessings" is found only and profusely in the prediction concerning Joseph.

2. In the same text we encounter the Hebrew *'olam* (everlasting) which is usually connected throughout Genesis with the covenants and the blessings of the promise. The importance of this is further corroborated in that the phrase "the eternal mountains, the bounties of the everlasting (*'olam*) hills" uttered by Jacob has a close counterpart in Moses' blessing: "the finest produce of the ancient mountains, and the abundance of the everlasting (*'olam*) hills." This indicates that God's will is ultimately carried through Joseph, not only at the end of Genesis but also at the end of the entire Torah (the Pentateuch).

3. In Moses' blessings, we can clearly see that Joseph, through his sons, Manasseh and Ephraim, will form the heart of Israel, both numerically and in matter of importance. This will be seen later especially in the Book of Judges. Furthermore, both Joshua and Samuel were Ephraimites (Josh 24:29-30; Judg 2:8-9; 1 Sam 1:1-2, 20).

Yet, practically speaking, Joseph will "disappear" from the picture and his two sons will supplant him as part of the "twelve tribes." Jacob will adopt Manasseh and Ephraim as his own (And Jacob said to Joseph... "And now your two sons, who were born to you in the earth of Egypt before I came to you in Egypt, are

mine; Ephraim and Manasseh shall be mine, as Reuben and
Simeon are"; Gen 48:3, 5). Consequently, the Joseph tribe will
receive double allotment, one for Manasseh and one for
Ephraim:

> For Moses had given an inheritance to the two and one-half tribes
> beyond the Jordan; but to the Levites he gave no inheritance
> among them. For the people of Joseph were two tribes, Manasseh
> and Ephraim; and no portion was given to the Levites in the earth,
> but only cities to dwell in, with their pasture lands for their cattle
> and their substance. (Josh 14:3-4)

> The people of Joseph, Manasseh and Ephraim, received their
> inheritance… Then allotment was made to the tribe of Manasseh,
> for he was the first-born of Joseph… Then Joshua said to the
> house of Joseph, to Ephraim and Manasseh, "You are a numerous
> people, and have great power; you shall not have one lot only"
> (16:4; 17:1, 17)[1]

Abraham's legacy was linked to the promise that produced
Isaac, the true heir promised by God. Similarly, here Joseph
"remained" without progeny to carry on his legacy, since his
children were adopted by Jacob. Yet, only he of all the brothers
was set to repose in Canaan. The bones of Joseph were preserved
for four hundred years and carried out of Egypt to the earth of
Canaan, a place he left unwillingly, being forced to do so by his
own brothers:

> And Joseph said to his brothers, "I am about to die; but God will
> visit you, and bring you up out of this earth to the earth which he
> swore to Abraham, to Isaac, and to Jacob." Then Joseph took an
> oath of the sons of Israel, saying, "God will visit you, and you shall
> carry up my bones from here." So Joseph died, being a hundred

---

[1] See also Num 1:32-35; 2:18-21; 10:22-23; 13, 8 and 11; 26:28-37.

and ten years old; and they embalmed him, and he was put in a coffin in Egypt. (Gen 50:24-26)

And Moses took the bones of Joseph with him; for Joseph had solemnly sworn the people of Israel, saying, "God will visit you; then you must carry my bones with you from here." (Ex 13:19)

The bones of Joseph which the people of Israel brought up from Egypt were buried at Shechem, in the portion of ground which Jacob bought from the sons of Hamor the father of Shechem for a hundred pieces of money; it became an inheritance of the descendants of Joseph. (Josh 24:32)

Joseph's meteoric "success," through God's providence, is presented as being indeed "complete." In spite of his death, he is presented as having survived the plan of Pharaoh to obliterate not only his family but the memory of him as well. This is to say, Joseph's story does not end in Genesis but continues through the exodus—through the trek in the wilderness where virtually all his "brethren" were relegated into oblivion by God himself and where Moses himself found his end—until finally his bones are brought to rest in the earth of the promise made to Abraham. Thus, if Isaac functions as the true heir of Abraham, Joseph functions as the true Abrahamide, the one who is of the kind of Abraham. Whereas even Isaac himself has a *toledot* (human generation, descendants; Gen 25:19) which includes Jacob whose life is replete with sins against God's will, Joseph's story, like only that of the forefather Abraham, is not introduced in scripture as a *toledot*, that is, a human story controlled by begetting.[2] The intention is clear: in both cases, the "continual" presence of the person is not through "human begetting" but rather through God's intervention.

---

[2] As a reminder, the Hebrew *toledot* is from the verbal root *yalad* (bear, bring forth, beget) the way all mammals do.

In the case of Abraham, we have a clear cut situation. Isaac was born through God's promise and not through Abraham's seed, as Paul pointed out magisterially: "For it is written that Abraham had two sons, one by a slave and one by a free woman. But the son of the slave was born according to the flesh, the son of the free woman was through promise." (Gal 4:22-23)[3] The case of Joseph is handled in a different way. Though he himself begat two children, Manasseh and Ephraim (Gen 41:50-52), these were adopted by Jacob (Gen 48) and became two of Jacob's sons during the allotment of the earth (Josh 14:1-4). That is why, early on in the Book of Judges, "the house of Joseph" is very soon split into Manasseh and Ephraim, both of whom we hear about extensively throughout that book.

Consequently, the biblical stories of Abraham and Joseph are presented as hanging by God's word rather than by actions of human endeavor. Abraham's story culminates with Isaac who fully inherits the earth of God's promise. Joseph's story, on the other hand, does not follow the same path. However, the story line is complete. It starts with a forced exile into Egypt and continues there with a full success when everyone expected complete failure. Moreover, this success is depicted as a realization of the promise to Abraham (Gen 12:1-3): Joseph, who was taken away from "his country and his kindred and his father's house" proves to be a blessing for Egypt as well as his own people. Then, after his sons are adopted by Jacob and thus after he was, as it were, disinherited of his human *toledot*, he—in his bones—finds final rest in the earth of promise (Josh 24:32) before that earth was brought under God's curse (Judg 2:11-15). Thus, Joseph's story, like Isaac's, is a story of full success from

---

[3] See my comments on these verses in *Gal* 238-242.

beginning to end *in spite of all adversities.* Joseph combines in his person the personalities of both Abraham and Isaac.

Judah and Tamar

The inclusion of an episode in the life of Judah (Gen 38) *within* the framework of the larger unit dealing with the cycle of Joseph (Gen 36-50) has consistently puzzled scholars and interpreters. Why does it not appear earlier with the episode concerning the behavior of Simeon and Levi toward the inhabitants of Shechem (Gen 34)? Why does it "interrupt" the Joseph cycle? Clearly it is intended to contrast Joseph with Judah, the father of the tribe whence originated the Davidic dynasty that wrought havoc and brought about disaster, destruction, and exile upon Jerusalem and its kingdom. This episode is introduced here to connect Judah's failures with Joseph's success in having secured the survival of his people in Egypt for more than 400 years. The story of Judah and Tamar presages, in a way, the story of David's household. Suffice it to point out here that the woman whose predicament was connected to her being the wife of two sons of Judah bears the name Tamar, the same name as David's daughter whose predicament was related to two of his sons and started the internecine fights within David's house. In both cases, the apparently decent houses of Judah and David hid a mound of sinfulness and self-righteousness. Although rejected later in favor of Judah (Ps 78:66-67), Joseph remains the one through whom and in whom God fulfills his promise. In this sense, Joseph functions, as Isaac before him, as a figure of the Suffering Servant of Isaiah whom God raised to show the way to salvation for those who were in exile in Babylon due to the sin of the Davidic dynasty, the kings of Judah.

From Joseph to Moses

The personality of Joseph as savior of his people prepares for
that of Moses as lawgiver for that same people. Ultimately,
Joseph's protection for Israel lasted only so long as the Pharaohs
remembered him. As soon as "there arose a new king over Egypt,
who did not know Joseph" (Ex 1:8) that protection turned
ineffective (vv.9-11). God will have to intervene again to save the
people. However, in order to erect a permanent fence of
protection around them, he institutes his Law inscribed in
writing for the ages, which will be the reflection of his gracious
presence and wisdom among them. If the wisdom of Joseph
protected his brothers and their children for some time, the
wisdom of the Law "written with the finger of God (himself)"
(Ex 30:18; Deut 9:10) will prove to be the guide of their
children's children for the ages. Thus, just as his name entails
(the Lord will add), Joseph, in spite of his greatness, is a mere
preamble to Moses, whose activity will cover four books. Even
more, Moses is the true leader who will lend his name to the five
books of the Law (known also as Moses)[4] one of which is
Genesis. It is as though in order to learn about Joseph and
anyone else before him, for that matter, one is to go through
Moses: "Tell me, you who desire to be under law, *do you not hear
the law? For it is written that Abraham had two sons*, one by a
slave and one by a free woman." (Gal 4:21-22)

The Book of Genesis starts with the issue of the knowledge of
the good and the evil and its misguided solution by the human
being (Gen 2-3). The same book ends with a solution to that
issue from God's perspective:

---

[4] 2 Cor 3:15 (Yes, to this day whenever Moses is read a veil lies over their minds).

When Joseph's brothers saw that their father was dead, they said, "It may be that Joseph will hate us and pay us back for all the *evil* which we did to him." So they sent a message to Joseph, saying, "Your father gave this command before he died, 'Say to Joseph, Forgive, I pray you, the transgression of your brothers and their sin, because they did *evil* to you.' And now, we pray you, forgive the transgression of the servants of the God of your father." Joseph wept when they spoke to him. His brothers also came and fell down before him, and said, "Behold, we are your servants." But Joseph said to them, "Fear not, for am I in the place of God? As for you, you meant *evil* against me; but God meant it for *good*, to bring it about that many people should be kept alive, as they are today. (Gen 50:15-20)

At the beginning of Genesis *the man* (*ha'adam*) and his children failed to understand that the right solution to the issue of the good and the evil does not lie in our choice, but rather that the good lies in our obedience to God's commandment itself, which obedience ensures the perpetual enjoyment of the fruit of the tree of life. That is why the divine perspective on the good and the evil offered at the end of Genesis will be spelled out in the Law containing detailed commandments which are "holy and just and *good*" (Rom 7:12) so much so that, though the Law is issued specifically to Israel, it is ultimately intended for every human being as the way toward true and full life:

All the commandment which I command you this day you shall be careful to do, that you may live and multiply, and go in and possess the land which the Lord swore to give to your fathers. And you shall remember all the way which the Lord your God has led you these forty years in the wilderness, that he might humble you, testing you to know what was in your heart, whether you would keep his commandments, or not. And he humbled you and let you hunger and fed you with manna, which you did not know, nor did your fathers know; that he might make you know that *the man* (*ha'adam*) does not live by bread alone, but that *the man* (*ha'adam*) lives by everything that proceeds out of the mouth of the Lord. (Deut 8:1-3)

Further Reading

Commentaries and Studies

John Chrysostom, *Homilies on Genesis 1-17*, The Fathers of the Church, Vol. 74, Robert C. Hill, translator. Washington, D.C.: Catholic University of America Press.

John Chrysostom, *Homilies on Genesis 18-45*, The Fathers of the Church, Vol. 82, Robert C. Hill, translator. Washington, D.C.: Catholic University of America Press.

John Chrysostom, *Homilies on Genesis 46-67*, The Fathers of the Church, Vol. 87, Robert C. Hill, translator. Washington, D.C.: Catholic University of America Press.

Brodie, T. L. *Genesis as Dialogue: A Literary, Historical, and Theological Commentary.* Oxford: Oxford University Press, 2001.

Davies, P. R. and Clines, D. J. A. *The World of Genesis: Persons, Places, Perspectives.* Sheffield: Sheffield Academic Press, 1998.

Hess, R. S. *Studies in the Personal Names of Genesis 1-11.* Kevalaer: Butzon & Becker; Neukirchener: Neukirchen-Vlyun, 1993. The meaning of names is important for a literary reading of the genealogies and narratives.

Kaltner, J. *Inquiring of Joseph: Getting to Know a Biblical Character through the Qur'an.* Interfaces. Collegeville, MN: Liturgical Press, 2003.

Kessler, M. and Deurloo, K. *A Commentary on Genesis: The Book of Beginnings.* Mahwah, NJ: Paulist Press, 2004.

McKeown, J. *Genesis.* Two Horizons Old Testament Commentary. Grand Rapids, MI: Eerdmans, 2008. Commentary followed by discussions of themes.

Noort, E. and Tigghelaar, E. (eds.) *The Sacrifice of Isaac: The Aqedah and Its Interpretations.* Leiden: Brill, 2002.

Scullion, J. J., S.J. *Genesis: A Commentary for Students, Teachers, and Preachers.* Old Testament Studies, vol.6. Collegeville, MN: The Liturgical Press, 1992.

Turner, L. A. *Genesis.* Readings: A New Biblical Commentary. Sheffield: Sheffield Academic Press, 2000. Deals with Genesis as a literary unit and underscores the narrative plot.

Wénin, A. (ed.) *Studies in the Book of Genesis: Literature, Redaction and History.* Leuven: Leuven University Press, 2001.

Articles

Clifford, R. J., S.J. "Genesis 38: Its Contribution to the Jacob Story." *Catholic Biblical Quarterly* 66 (2004) 519-532.

Davila, J. "The Flood Hero as King and Priest." *Journal of Near Eastern Studies.* 54 (1995) 199-214.

Dozemann, T. B. "The Wilderness and Salvation History in the Hagar Story." *Journal of Biblical Literature* 117 (1998) 23-43.

Eslinger, L. "The enigmatic plurals like 'one of us' (Genesis i 26, iii 22, and xi 7) in hyperchronic perspective." *Vetus Testamentum* 56 (2006) 171-184.

Goldingay, J. "The Significance of Circumcision." *Journal for the Study of the Old Testament* 88 (2000) 3-18. Discussion of Genesis 17.

McKeown, J. "The Theme of Land in Genesis 1-11 and its Significance for the Abraham Narrative." *Irish Biblical Studies* 19 (1997) 51-64.

McKeown, J. "The Theme of Land in Genesis 1-11 and its Significance for the Abraham Narrative. (Part II)." *Irish Biblical Studies* 19 (1997) 133-44.

Noble, P. R. "Esau, Tamar, and Joseph: Criteria for identifying inner-biblical allusions." *Vetus Testamentum* 52 (2002) 219-252.

Tonson P. "Mercy without Covenant: A Literary Analysis of Genesis 19." *Journal for the Study of the Old Testament* 95 (2001) 95-116.

Sparks, K. "Genesis 49 and the Tribal List Tradition in Ancient Israel." *Zeitschrift für die Alttestamentliche Wissenschaft* 115 (2003) 327-347.

Wénin, A. "L'histoire de Joseph (Genèse 37-50)." *Cahier Evangile* 130 (2004) 1-55.

Wilder, W. N. "Illumination and Investiture: The Royal Significance of the Tree of Wisdom in Genesis 3." *The Westminster Theological Journal* 68 (2006) 51-69.

Breinigsville, PA USA
10 February 2011
255238BV00001B/15/P